Collector's Encyclopedia of

SALT GLAZE STONEWARE

Identification & Value Guide

Terry Taylor and Terry and Kay Lowrance

COLLECTOR BOOKS

A Division of Schroeder Publishing Co., Inc.

The current values in this book should be used only as a guide. They are not intended to set prices, which vary from one section of the country to another. Auction prices as well as dealer prices vary greatly and are affected by condition as well as demand. Neither the Authors nor the Publisher assumes responsibility for any losses that might be incurred as a result of consulting this guide.

Searching For A Publisher?

We are always looking for knowledgeable people considered to be experts within their fields. If you feel that there is a real need for a book on your collectible subject and have a large comprehensive collection, contact Collector Books.

On the Cover: Clockwise from top center (mint values for each):

Eagle pitcher, blue and white, $600.00 – 800.00;
Grazing Cows pitcher, green and cream, $250.00 – 300.00;
Lion's Head soap dish, blue and white, $150.00 – 200.00;
Wildflower rolling pin with advertising, blue and white, $500.00 – 600.00;
Peacock pitcher, blue and white, $600.00 – 800.00.

Cover Design: Karen Geary
Book Design: Benjamin R. Faust
Cover Photo: Terry Taylor

Additional copies of this book may be ordered from:

COLLECTOR BOOKS
P.O. Box 3009
Paducah, KY 42002-3009

@ $24.95. Add $2.00 for postage and handling.

Printed in the U.S.A. by Image Graphics

Contents

Preface

We are obsessive collectors. It has become a passion and a love. All collectors know about this fervor and wonder where it will end. Should this obsession be classified as an illness, no one seems to be looking for a cure nor do we really want to find one.

The term "salt glaze" is readily used when describing these pieces. Because of its common use as a term for this colorful molded stoneware, it can be endorsed as a generic name for these pieces of "factory made" wares. Call it what you want — it's old, it's beautiful, and it should be preserved and appreciated. It is a collectible deserving an appropriate place in American pottery history. We wish for you many happy and fulfilling pursuits.

References cited throughout the text are listed in the End Notes at the close of the book.

Acknowledgments

Without the kind generosity of a number of individuals sharing their expertise on the subject and their collections for photographing, this assemblage of information regarding colors, shapes, and values of molded stoneware, or salt glaze as we fondly call it, would not have been possible. The true love and revelry of these mementos of a bygone era transcended the risk of our unknown faces to create a lasting work honoring the beauty of these treasures from the past. Many, many thanks are extended to these individuals for allowing our intrusion into their homes during this endeavor.

All examples shown are from the collections of the authors, Terry and Kay Lowrance and Terry Taylor, as well as the following molded stoneware enthusiasts to whom we are most grateful:

Ted and Sandra Gleason
Charlie and Peggy Gray
Earl and Marie Kearns
Blaine and Gloria Piper
Gary and Debbie Thompson
Jimmy and Cecil Waddell

Introduction

Ever since the Industrial Revolution altered the process of manufacturing goods by allowing for mass production, history has recorded the plight of businesses to keep up with the constantly inventive nature of our own American society as well as that of the rest of the world. Not only were massive machines and production methods the result of inventors' creativity, but also quite simple utilitarian household wares were the consequence of creative minds.

Potters, resting upon the spartan yet dependable wheel for shaping from a clump of clay the variety of jugs, crocks, and bowls needed since ancient times for the storage, preservation, and preparation of food, suddenly had their livelihoods threatened by revolutionary manufacturing processes as well as by the variety of new products which resulted. By the mid 1800s, the glass food storage jar, i.e., the Mason jar, was beginning to attract a share of the market which potters had enjoyed. By the late 1800s glass was widely used for a variety of purposes including food storage and preservation.

The elegance of the Victorian era led consumers to disenchantment with the dull, plain forms of utilitarian housewares which were available to the common person who could not afford the finer porcelains and ceramics most notably produced in England. By the mid 1800s the use of molds had been introduced for the mass production of a variety of everyday household wares.[15] Rather than giving an item its form on the potter's wheel, clay was pressed into molds for the formation of wares. Even with this new technology, the resulting products remained somewhat plain with the preferred yellow clay used for production being sealed with clear glazes and occasionally decorated quite simply with bands of color. Yellow ware, as it has become generically known, became a direct competitor with the potter's wheel as well as glass container production.

With the progression of the Victorian era and the discovery of natural clay resources during the westward movement in the United States, the more enterprising potteries linked changing consumer preferences to the molding process using locally abundant clay to secure a niche in the production of utilitarian housewares which lasted well into the next century. Realizing that hand-thrown wares were technologically obsolete, progressively thinking potteries as well as new entrepreneurs ingeniously applied molding techniques to embellish plainly produced products to generate common, inexpensive, utilitarian wares sculpted to meet the desires and tastes of their customers.

Using plentiful white clays pressed into an almost endless array of patterned molds, applying color for decoration, and glazing the completed product, potteries found transition to the next generation of stoneware. The golden era of molded stoneware dominated the market for everyday household wares from about 1890 until the mid 1930s. Just as the Mason jar assisted in the demise of numerous potteries, the continued growth of the glass industry and other modern conveniences such as "indoor plumbing" brought about the demise of many molded stoneware producers between 1930 and the mid 1950s. And so, just as the glass industry felt secure with its market niches for utilitarian housewares, plastics became the material of choice for modern-day pouring, storage, and preserving containers.

Since mechanization revolutionized product manufacturing, each era has seen a trail of discards abandoned in favor of more modern conveniences. While the pursuit of any discard provides a challenge for today's collector, it is our intent to assist you in your own "Pursuit of Molded Stoneware" by helping you to identify the shapes, colors, and values. These wares from a bygone era are now recognized for their artistry even though they were originally produced very inexpensively for everyday usage and were never intended for decorative purposes.

Molds and Shapes

By simply adding decorative elements to create a three-dimensional effect, molded wares were transformed from very plain to quite fancy. "Sculptures" of whole items provided the original from which two-part molds were cast using plaster-like material. Each half of the two-part mold provided the pattern for the exterior of the finished product. Although not always true, patterns were typically the same on both sides of the finished product. Since the molds were used for quantity production, they did become worn which resulted in finished products with less than distinct patterns. Clarity of the pattern is often used as a criterion of current collectors in determining the value of the collectible, and "first-out-of-the-mold" pieces, as they are often described, can command higher prices.

Clay collected from abundant local deposits was delivered and readied at the pottery from which the jiggermen could select material for each day's production. As Forrest Poston writes, "To start the day, each jiggerman had to select a wagon load of clay, looking for the right feel for the day's project. Clay had been molded into cakes from which the jiggerman cut the proper thickness for the job. While the cutting was partially mechanized, getting the thickness right depended strictly on the jiggerman's eye."[14]

Clay sliced to the correct thickness for the items being produced was then pressed into each mold half. Once removed from the molds, the two halves were joined to form the whole piece. Wet sponges were used to smooth the seams where the two halves were joined. Some patterns creatively used columns, trees, etc., on the seams to camouflage them. Because these wares were mass produced for everyday usage, seams were not always cleaned with precision. Poston explains that new hires often performed the "mold boy" tasks of carting molds from one part of the factory to another and hand-rolling handles in between.[14]

Handles, sometimes molded separately and sometimes formed by hand, were applied after the two halves were joined. Pouring spouts were often a part of the mold while on some pieces, pouring lips were pulled and formed from the clay rim of a pitcher. If not a part of the mold, knobs or finials were molded separately and then applied in the same manner as handles.

Production depended upon the creativity of mold makers who searched for new patterns and types of wares to which the molding process could be applied. Household items were the overwhelming focus of molded stoneware production. From kithenwares such as bowls, pitchers, rolling pins, mugs, butter holders, and salt crocks to sanitation items such as washbowls, pitchers, chamber pots, cuspidors, soap dishes, and umbrella stands, the molding of clay into a variety of wares having utility around the house seemed almost limitless.

On most pieces, there is usually an unglazed area, typically a raised rim around the bottom. Bowls often have fully glazed bottoms while the top rim and bottom side of the collar are unglazed. Lids are either unglazed on the interior side or have an unglazed band on the exterior side. Unglazed areas helped eliminate bonding of pieces in the fully loaded kiln. Glazed areas would bond when making contact with another item; unglazed rims, bands, or collars could make contact with another unglazed area or the ceramic kiln shelf without bonding. Butter holders having lipped lids, for example, could be fired with the lid on the holder since an unglazed raised rim would come in contact only with the unglazed interior of the lid. When an item was totally glazed, it had to be placed on three ceramic stilts in the kiln which usually left a slight, triangular indention in the piece. Bowls of the same size could be stacked quite high in a kiln since the unglazed rim of one could be placed inverted on the unglazed collar of another.

There were many companies in business during the boom years for molded stoneware. Some of the more well-known companies included:

Burley-Winter Pottery Company, Crooksville, Ohio
Brush-McCoy Pottery Company, Zanesville, Ohio
Logan Pottery Company, Logan, Ohio
North Star Stoneware Company, Red Wing, Minnesota
Red Wing Union Stoneware Company, Red Wing, Minnesota
Ruckels Stoneware Company, Monmouth, Illinois
Star Stoneware Company, Akron, Ohio
Robinson Clay Pottery Company, Akron, Ohio
Western Stoneware Company, Monmouth, Illinois
Uhl Pottery Company, Huntingburg, Indiana

Identification of a particular maker can be difficult. While some of the companies marked a few of their wares, like Uhl, Red Wing, Star, and North Star, many more were unmarked. Red Wing is well known for producing advertising pieces. The block style ads on their wares as well as some of their catchy slogans help to identify a Red Wing piece.[3]

Patterns and Colors

Many different patterns were created for molded stoneware, some of which were used on pieces ranging from kitchen to sanitation, such as the Basketweave and Morning Glory pattern. Other patterns were apparently designed for a particular piece, such as the Daisy on Snowflake pattern which is seen solely on salt holders or the Currants and Diamonds pattern which was used primarily on bowls. Certain patterns were applied solely to kitchenwares, such as the Peacock pattern being used on pitchers, salt holders, butter crocks, bowls, and coffee pots, thus allowing the coordination of utilitarian pieces receiving everyday usage. Other patterns were exclusive to sanitation pieces such as the Fishscale and Wild Roses washstand sets consisting of a washbowl, pitcher, hot water pitcher, toothbrush holder, soap dish, powder box, and chamber pot. The Stenciled Wildflower is an example of a pattern seen on kitchenwares as well as sanitation pieces.

There were numerous patterns of molded stoneware as evidenced by the index at the end of this book which lists more than 150 patterns used on a variety of items. There are also many variations in the names given to the patterns. Common names were given to everyday scenes which grace many of the pieces. For example, the scene of cows grazing in what appears to be a field is commonly called "Grazing Cows." Other than some manufacturers' catalogs, no known official listing of patterns exists; however, with time, titles have been attached to pieces. Slightly different, although similar, variations in titles from what is listed may be seen according to geographical location.

Although mass-produced using a molding process rather than handmade on a potter's wheel, each piece usually has its own distinct characteristics and different shades of color. The coloration of some patterns is characteristically pale while others may have been produced in a single color only and still others in

multiple colors. In addition to mold patterns, many pieces were decorated or accented with color which was often applied to certain areas of the piece for highlighting or focusing. Color highlightings were typically diffused, meaning that the color faded from the area of focus toward the natural color. Color was often added to plain and patterned forms with sponging decoration.

Interiors most often have a white Bristol glaze. Bristol glaze contains zinc oxide which gives it a white color. There are many shades of white and some are quite gray or yellowish, depending on the purity of the particular clay and the amount of zinc oxide used. This interior white glazing was a change from earlier handmade potter's wheel stoneware which usually had Albany Slip interiors. Slip is a mixture of refined clay, usually dark reddish or brown that was used as a sealant on the interiors of the early wares to prevent liquids from leaching into the clay or contamination from the clay from seeping into the stored food. The reddish color came from the amount of iron in the clay.[3]

The cobalt blue in blue and white stoneware is a metallic oxide that comes in a powder form which is mixed into a thin solution of white Bristol glaze. The main reason so many wares were produced in blue and white is that the blue cobalt oxide was the only oxide that was stable and predictable under the high firing temperatures used in producing the wares. The other oxides, iron for red and some yellows, copper oxide for green, and manganese for browns and blacks, were unpredictable. Using the other oxides sometimes resulted in odd colors and patterns and occasionally, they broke down completely.[3]

Today's collector finds many pieces to be quite elegant not only in form and design but also in the variety of colors in which molded stoneware was produced, including the appealing blue and white, as well as green and cream, yellow, and brown. These distinct, vibrant colors appeal to many collectors.

By far the most prevalent color is some form of blue. There were many shades of blue depending on the clay and cobalt oxide reaction. Although less frequently seen, green and cream pieces typically command prices 25 – 50 percent less than their blue counterparts. Items and patterns which were produced in blue may never have been produced in green or other colors. Yet, many pieces were produced in a variety of colors.

Brown pieces generally do not command the same prices as blue or green items. Brown pitchers are the most typical finds. Other pieces such as butters, salts, etc., in browns and other combinations are uncommonly seen. Brown pieces are sometimes referred to as tomorrow's collectible, meaning that the brown color may someday reach the popularity of blue and white.

There also are color combinations, such as a half green and half brown Flying Birds pitcher, and Cow pitcher, which some people feel were experiments with glazes. These combinations were not produced in mass, and although they are considered rare in most cases, prices generally are in line with other colors and do not reflect the rarity.

Spotting Repairs, Reproductions, and Married Pieces

As with most popular antiques and collectibles, reproductions have also infiltrated the molded stoneware field. Through trial and error, talking with collectors, and by handling hundreds of pieces, one develops a certain amount of expertise that may help in identifying suspect pieces. Be suspicious of a piece if it is totally pristine — no flakes, chips, pits, hairline fractures, crazing, etc. In general, the following tips for identifying the "real thing" versus a reproduction should prove valuable:

1. Use the "crystal test," as it is aptly referred to by William Daggett. Set a piece in the palm of your hand and gently flick your index fingernail against its rim as if flicking a piece of crystal for its resonating ring. If you hear that nice "ting" sound similar to crystal or cut glass when it is tapped, be suspect of its age. When flicking old stoneware, you will typically hear a nice "thud" or muffled sound with no high pitch. Be aware that this is not a foolproof test as some old pieces in pristine condition may have a "ting" sound. Likewise, some reproductions may have been aged with crazing, dirt, and even hairline fractures any of which may reduce the "tinging" sound. This is also referred to as the "thumper test" since, when an old item is thumped, it will emit a thud or a low, deep sound. If the piece "pings" or makes a high-pitched sound, it may be a reproduction and should be subjected to further examination.[3]

2. Inspect indentations on the interior of the mold as a clue to reproductions, particularly on pitchers where the handles connect to the body and where exterior patterns protrude. With the old pieces there will be a smooth, flat surface with no indentation on the interior since enough clay would have been pressed into the mold to fill the protruding areas. Handles were typically hand-formed or molded and applied separately rather than made as a part of the body of the item.

Frequently reproduced pieces presently seen include the Grazing Cows pitcher, Eagle pitcher, Lovebirds pitcher, Indian in War Bonnet pitcher, Sleepy Eye pitchers, various salt holders, and soap dishes. Not many soap dishes were made, and they were susceptible to breakage, so, few good examples survive.[3]

3. Apply the "smell test" to grease and butter crocks as a possible indicator of authenticity since well-used examples will typically smell rancid.

4. Check lids to be sure they are a match in pattern. An exact color match is of lesser importance since lids were commonly fired separately; therefore, different shades in color are acceptable. Be aware of "married" pieces where pastry, butter, or salt crock lids have been mismatched with the bottom half. The

examples shown generally have the matching lids unless noted otherwise It is hoped that this emphasis will make the collector more aware of proper container-lid mates.

5.   Learn to identify an original bail since it increases the value of a piece. The center grip is usually unpainted wood which has a natural patina acquired only over a period of time, or it may be painted black which should also show wear. New replacement center grips are also usually painted black; thus, caution should be taken.

6.   Look carefully for signs of repair, especially on pitcher spouts and handles. Paint is commonly used to conceal minor repairs. Some paint matches are excellent and hardly noticeable. If a piece is very rare and the repair is good, do not unnecessarily dismiss the purchase. Of course, the price should be in line with the damage and the repair not misrepresented by the seller.

7.   Look for attempted aging or "dirtying." This terminology means using dirt to make a piece look old. Some pieces look as if they have been buried in garden soil for a while in order to age the reproduction.

8.   Look for crazing, the fine spiderweb-like lines that sometimes develop in glazes as a sign of age. Most old crazing is true to form and is hard to reproduce. While there are many pristine examples of molded stoneware, keep in mind that the ware was utilitarian and most pieces should show some aspect of wear and/or age since many are 60 to 75 or more years old. While crazing can be reproduced, old crazing just looks different from newly imposed crazing. New crazing tends to show an overall effect while old crazing may appear only in certain areas, like the bottom interiors of pitchers or exterior areas of the glaze. Ask an experienced collector to show you an example of crazing from his or her collection.

Molded stoneware is a very durable product. While the clay may be quite delicate, the glaze is not. The glaze is virtually impervious to artificial attempts to make it appear old — even scouring pads can be used to clean it without leaving a scratch. Thus, be apprehensive about pieces which have rough textures; the original glaze is typically smooth and actually has its own natural shine.[3]

9.   Look for "runs" in the glazes, especially on the inside. These runs can be a sign of an old piece.

10.   Lift a piece to check its weight since older pieces, especially pitchers, are typically heavier than reproductions. Weight of a piece, however, is not foolproof. Handle as much pottery as possible and you will begin to acquire the right feel for an old piece.

11.   Look for hairline cracks and chips since they are normal signs of use which in turn indicates age. Consider the purchase if you do not already have the item; it could be a long time before you see another, and, if the piece is very rare, a perfect one may never come your way again. If it does, you can always trade up.

12.   Ask to see a potential purchase in bright light or, even better, sunlight where possible, so that you can evaluate the item more clearly, keeping the aforementioned tips in mind.

13.   Establish a return policy should a repair or a reproduction be discovered after the purchase. Be sure that you know how to contact the dealer. Once at home, subject the piece to a thorough washing. Methods that expose repairs, especially paint repairs, are to wash the piece in the dishwasher and/or soak the item overnight in a sink filled with water and one cup of bleach. Either of these methods will not only expose repairs, but will also assist in cleaning. These methods will not damage the piece.

14.   Inspect pieces for dried paint specks occurring from a careless painter who may not have moved items when painting a room. These speckles may be a sign of age.

Acceptable Replacements and Repairs

As advocated earlier, any repairs, additions or cover-ups should be clearly marked if a piece is for sale. It is also a good idea for collectors to identify repairs on a sticker placed on the bottom of a piece for future reference since, as your collection grows, you may tend to forget.

Lids are notoriously missing from certain pieces, such as salt holders, butter crocks, and chamberpots. While missing parts do detract from the mint value of a piece, an item should not be totally discounted from consideration since a matching "orphan" companion may one day be found. Never turn down a perfect salt holder just because the lid is missing. A round wooden lid with an appropriate knob finial is very pleasing and can easily be made. They look very seasoned when stained appropriately, and you may want to woodwork several for future lidless finds. Wooden lids will also work on such items as canisters. If a lid has minor repairs, such as a glued together section, do not consider it that negatively, especially if the piece is rare.

Be sure to check the lid for a correct match in patterns. Although lids were always made separately and glazes some-times differed in color, the pattern should match. "Married" pieces, meaning mismatched lids, are sometimes seen for sale in an effort to fool a novice collector. These pieces are usually being offered as perfect at a higher price than they would bring otherwise.

Wire wooden-handled bails are often missing from butter holders; thus, replacements are common, acceptable, and available. Most new bails have a wooden center grip painted black. These additions do not necessarily lessen the value of a piece, but rather contribute to restoring the original condition for appealing display. Bails can be acquired from dealers in the wares at flea markets or through suppliers who advertise in antique trade publications or through collector societies. One current source of bails is through Andy Hebenstreit. For a price list, mail a self-addressed stamped envelope to him at 607 Carrington, Waupun, WI 53953 (telephone: 414/324-2525).

Bails can also be fashioned from an old piece of heavy wire. Handles from old gas or oil cans with a perfect old wooden grip can often be used to fashion a wire bail replacement.

Cleaning Molded Stoneware

First, examine the piece to determine the extent of cleaning needed. A simple rinse with a grease-cutting dishwashing liquid may be all that is needed. Any washing job should be done carefully with a rubber mat in the sink to protect the piece in case it should slip from your hands.

After washing the piece, it is good to set it out to air dry. Be sure the piece is thoroughly dry. Since some bottoms are not completely glazed, the porous clay can absorb moisture that could leave a watermark on furniture where the piece is set.

Sometimes a more thorough cleaning is needed. In these cases, try a scouring powder cleanser. Wet the piece, sprinkle it with the cleanser, and work it into a paste consistency as you gently rub it with your hand. In severe cases, you may have to let the piece soak in the paste for a while. Keep the paste moist by laying a wet towel over it. Stubborn dirt can be removed with a soapy scouring pad available in the house cleaning products area of your grocery store. You may also encounter old, encrusted food deposits that require the closer attention of a knife or

scraper. When using the scouring pads or a knife, be careful not to damage the piece.

When tackling an extremely dirty piece, try placing the item in a mild bleach solution. It may take time and additional bleach to do the job so be prepared to exhibit patience in the soaking and scouring processes. The aforementioned treatment of adding additional bleach is not recommended except in extreme cases where the piece is discolored with dirt, grime, or even rust. This method also can expose repairs as mentioned earlier.

Oven cleaner can also be used to remove stubborn baked-on debris. A good idea with oven cleaner, however, is to first test the cleaner on the bottom of the item.

When cleaning rolling pins, be careful not to damage the wooden handles. They can be removed to clean the pottery portion, but be careful not to force a handle that does not want to easily turn loose. Most have one end that screws onto the center rod or the handle is simply inserted onto the rod. The wooden part can be cleaned with a mild detergent or soap. Let the handle dry and then apply a coat of quality paste wax. Do not use a vegetable or cooking oil since these products are not intended to treat wood and will become rancid. Wooden handles that have been painted can be stripped and restored to the natural wood.

Always be on the lookout for a set of wooden handles that would work on a roller found without the "pin". Wooden rollers with nice handles can be found for a reasonable price and can sometimes provide a needed set of replacements If you find a pottery roller in good condition but without the pin and for a good price, buy it and make finding the pin an adventure!

One last note on cleaning methods concerns dealing with a piece which has lost its shiny glaze. The deteriorated gloss is not detrimental since these pieces are showing their use or may not have had a high gloss. When a piece lacks luster, a high quality lacquer or an oil product used by gun enthusiasts on wooden stocks may be sprayed on the pottery to provide a high gloss and a durable finish. After treatment such as this, the piece should not be used for food.

Pricing and Values

As with all antiques and collectibles, condition is a major factor in value. If you are collecting strictly for investment purposes, hold out for the pristine examples. Of course, be prepared to pay top dollar for those selections. Most pieces of molded stoneware have some minor flaws such as small chips, pits, hairline fractures, missing parts, broken lids, or crazing (small spiderweb-like cracks in the glaze). As long as there is no major damage such as distinct cracks or major chips, pieces may be acceptable if the price is right and especially for personal use as "shelf pieces." As long as one side displays well, these finds can accent decor nicely.

The price guide in this book serves only as a simple road map to let you know if you are in the ballpark for a fair market price. We have all paid too much for something we just had to have. You can probably remember those occasions at an auction when your bidding hand just could not be contained.

Molded stoneware can still be found at flea markets, auctions, antique malls, shows, and individual shops. Develop a discerning eye to quickly spot it. Personal collections are sometimes, but rarely, sold. Starting a collection is not difficult since one or two pieces will fit into almost any decorating scheme. The more common pieces can still be found at reasonable prices.

Price guides are often a factor in consulting any reference book for antiques and collectibles. Whether you consider it good or bad, prices for antiques have generally increased over the years and will probably continue to do so. True antiques and collectibles having value are hard to find and are typically priced accordingly. Molded stoneware is no exception since, as with all antiques, it becomes increasingly difficult to find.

The factors used in determining mint prices include the following:

Rarity — frequency with which an item is seen, in collections or for sale, which usually is relative to the number produced.

Condition — presence of any detrimental factors such as chips, fractures, or repairs.

Pattern clarity — mold pattern that is distinctly clear or faint.

Color — strength of the hue of a piece. Blue tends to be the color of choice, although green is often more difficult and challenging to find.

Popularity — some patterns by their nature are more popular than others. The Grazing Cows pitcher could be cited as an example because of its bovine appeal and decorating interest.

Age determination — indicators that a piece is truly old rather than a reproduction.

The prices in this book are recommended to be used only as a guide. Neither the authors nor the publisher assumes any responsibility for any losses that may occur as a result of consulting this guide. It is our opinion any item is only worth what you are willing to pay for it. Like all collectibles, we have paid too much for that piece we just had to have, and we have also made an occasional "steal" by paying much too little for something of far greater value.

Condition and Pricing Criteria

MINT — No chips, no flakes, no cracks, no hairline fractures, good distinct deep pattern, good coloration. Has all original parts such as lids, original wire bails, and handles. Glaze is shiny. Examples with these characteristics can command a higher-end market value comparable to those listed.

NEAR MINT — No chips, no flakes, no major cracks. Has distinct mold pattern, shiny glaze, good coloration, and original lids or component parts. One or two small hairline fractures are acceptable. Acceptable to have replaced wire bails and wooden handles. Examples with these characteristics will typically carry values which are 25 percent less than those listed.

GOOD — May have some of the following: small minor chips, small flakes, or hairline fractures. Should have distinct mold pattern and good coloration. Original lids may have some damage such as small minor chips, flakes, hairline fractures or may be missing entirely. Wire bails and handles may be missing or replacements. Values for examples having these characteristics are usually reduced by approximately 50 percent of those listed.

FAIR — Has major chip or flake of one-fourth inch or greater. May have a noticeable crack of three inches or longer. Mold pattern may be faint, denoting an older, used mold, and color may be pale as compared to an example with good coloration. Glaze may be dull and/or pitted. Examples in Fair condition will typically be valued at 60 percent less than the values listed.

POOR — Has major chips, cracks, repairs, and possible missing parts. Has faint mold pattern and/or bad coloration. Examples in poor condition will typically be priced 75 to 80 percent less than the values listed.

These Condition and Pricing Criteria serve as a guide in determining an appropriate value for examples found in various states from mint to poor. While quoted value ranges are for mint pieces, we all know that many examples found do not reflect that condition; thus, value is affected.

Availability Index

The following is a guide to the availability rating given to examples shown. Four general categories are used with one category typically given as an index of how frequently a collector may expect to locate a particular item. For certain items, greater clarification for the categorical rating is provided in terms of COLOR, SIZE, and/or PATTERN.

EXTREMELY RARE as a category means that an item is seen quite infrequently in private collections as well as for sale. A collector may conduct a long search to add an item with this rating to his or her collection, especially an item in mint condition. Certain COLORS, SIZES, and/or PATTERNS are often considered EXTREMELY RARE.

RARE as a category means that an item is neither commonly seen in private collections nor for sale. While items considered to be rare infrequently become available in the market, collectors can be less selective in that another example may not be found for quite some time. Certain examples may be classified as having RARE COLOR, being a RARE SIZE, and/or being a RARE PATTERN.

SCARCE as a category indicates that an item is occasionally seen in collections and for sale. Collectors may exercise some degree of selectivity; however, examples in less than mint condition may be acceptable. Price variations will exist for items in this category but to a lesser extent than for items being commonly available.

COMMON as a category indicates that an item is frequently seen in collections and for sale. Collectors can typically be quite selective in acquiring examples. Prices may vary considerably for items with this rating since they are more available and are typically in various states of condition.

In addition to the general availability index, specific characteristics may be noted about individual items. While a particular pattern may be rated as common, a certain color or size may be noted as rare. As an example, the Grazing Cows pattern for pitchers is rated as common; however, examples found in yellow are extremely rare and will thus be presented as follows:

AVAILABILITY: Common pattern
COLORS: Blue and white, green and cream, brown, yellow (extremely rare)

Living with Your Collection

Molded stoneware is traditionally a country motif decorating item. However, you can do a lot of things with the various pieces by mixing them with other similar items to give your home that personal, eclectic blend. Here are some ideas for consideration:

Nothing is more beautiful than an open or "blind door" cupboard filled with colorful stoneware. A cupboard like this also looks good with other "country" items mixed in, such as wooden butter molds and butter prints, a draped country linen, wooden red apples, bread boards, and other treenware.

Use a washbowl and pitcher set on an antique washstand. You can accent the display further with the complementing pieces such as a soap dish, toothbrush holder, and hot water pitcher.

Spongeware can take on a contemporary and/or Far Eastern look when displayed on a wooden base such as those used with Oriental bowls. A pot-bellied spongeware pitcher especially looks good displayed this way.

A large bowl can be used as a fruit bowl.

At your next party, take a large stoneware bowl, line it with cabbage leaves (maybe alternating green and purple) then fill the center with slaw or your favorite dip. A wooden spoon will complete the look. Very large stoneware bowls could also be used for serving punch.

Wooden red apples, red strawberries, or blackberries all complement the natural beauty of molded pottery. Another good idea is to take a couple of strands of wooden, cranberry-colored beads and circle them in a bowl for a "berry" look. These strands are sold during the Christmas holiday season as garland and are an inexpensive way to dress up a bowl in a festive motif.

Use a soap dish next to the kitchen sink or bath vanity. It can be used to hold decorative soaps, soap for everyday use, or maybe even potpourri.

A chamber pot looks good beside an antique bed as it was originally used.

A pitcher can be used as a vase for a bouquet of flowers. It is not suggested that you put water directly into a pitcher for a prolonged length of time since a leak may occur, resulting in a water circle on your furniture because of the porous clay. Place a glass jar or other inconspicuous container inside the pitcher. Dried flowers or stems of pussy willow also look good displayed in a pitcher.

Christmas is a great time to decorate with stoneware. Save sprigs cut from the bottom of your Christmas tree or favorite evergreen and create an arrangement using the glass insert method described above. Finish the look with some red berry sprigs tucked among the greens or add a festive bow to your creative endeavor.

An "orphan" washbowl can be set on a bath counter or floor and filled with rolled-up hand towels and wash cloths. Blue, burgundy, hunter green, and cream provide excellent complimentary colors for blue and white pottery pieces.

Butter crocks and salt holders are clever containers for tucking away small trinkets to which you need quick access, such as rubber bands and twist ties in a kitchen.

Display an "orphan" lid on a plate stand until you find a matched crock. The pattern can be easily seen and enjoyed.

A favorite pitcher can be kept on your kitchen counter to hold cooking utensils. A small roll of paper towels will also fit inside a large pitcher. Rotate the pitchers if you have several so that you can enjoy your favorite ones on a daily basis.

When entertaining, use a pitcher or two on your table to hold a favorite beverage. Also, for a special dinner, fill a butter crock with spreadable butter and a salt holder with salt for a nostalgic look.

When antiquing, look for and purchase other collectibles that will complement your stoneware collection. Appropriate accessories include tin cookie cutters, old kitchen items such as spoons, spatulas, measures, graniteware pans, and country linens. These are usually available at reasonable prices and help create an interesting "salt glaze" display.

It is recommended that you begin an inventory system through which you record your collection. An entry can be written in a log book including an inventory number, date of acquisition, description, price paid, and source. You may wish to go one step further by placing the inventory number on a sticker which, in most cases, can be placed out of sight on the bottom of the piece for a quick memory refresher. Other cataloging measures are also advisable for security, such as taking a current video or photos of your collection. It is further advised that you keep a copy of your up-to-date log in a location other than your home for security and insurance purposes.

Collector Organization

The "Blue and White Pottery Club" was organized in 1981. Membership includes a quarterly newsletter featuring free member advertising in a current buy, sell, and trade section; general news and feature articles on blue and white pottery; news articles from around the country submitted by club members; and information and locations of new and exciting antique shops, malls, and auctions throughout the country. Membership benefits also include an annual members-only convention each June in various locations in the Midwest. Convention activities include a blue and white stoneware pottery show, sale, and auction as well as room sales, a banquet, various educational workshops, and opportunities to meet other blue and white stoneware pottery collectors. While room sales and table sales may include colors other than blue and white, the focus of the convention, its workshops, and the auction is on blue and white stoneware only.

An added highlight for convention attendees is a blue and white commemorative which is a miniature version of a selected stoneware piece stamped with the convention year. These miniatures are collectible themselves and are available only to attendees of the convention.

The principal goals of the Blue and White Pottery Club are to share information, encourage learning, and foster an appreciation of the distinct history, wide variety, and increasing collectibility of blue and white stoneware pottery. Equally important goals are the promotion and nurturing of friendships with fellow collectors and providing equal opportunity for all to participate in new discoveries and exciting information about blue and white stoneware pottery.

Presently dues are $12 per year for one individual and an additional $5 per year for another family member. For more information about joining, contact:

Blue and White Pottery Club
c/o Mr. Howard Gardner
224 12th Street, NW
Cedar Rapids, Iowa 52405

From Whence the Pursuit Evolved

Even research yields little specific information about the history of molded stoneware. Sadly, most attention has been paid to the evolution of hand-thrown pottery making in America with all its trials and tribulations, and little attention has been devoted to the period after 1900 regarding molded stoneware. It has been documented that the molded stoneware focused upon in this book was produced predominantly after 1890 and replaced hand-thrown pottery in terms of mass production.

Yet, the meaningfulness of today's molded stoneware pursuits has its roots in those eras having received greatest research attention, and thus, it is important to briefly examine from whence our current pursuits have evolved.

A "history" is, at best, what one thinks happened during a period of time based on the facts available. The purpose here is not to present a complete history of pottery making in America, but rather to give readers an idea of where this molded stoneware collectible fits in the overall history of pottery making. For more thorough treatment of this evolution, the end notes offer a number of excellent works on the subject.

Prior to the development of new methods of forming clay and new glazing techniques in the early industrialization of pottery making, virtually all pottery made in America was what can best be defined as folk pottery. Folk potters were highly skilled. They used simple materials readily available to them and produced simple designs to meet utilitarian needs of simple people. Every piece was produced for a particular function.[8]

During each era of history and for each classification of pottery, various types and grades were made, finished, and glazed. Most consumers had little choice but to buy what wares were produced in their local areas.

Earthenware was one of the first types of pottery made. It was produced from about 1640 to the end of the colonial period around 1781. Earthenware was made in many regions because of the abundance of the red clay that required low firing temperatures. One of the first types is known as red ware, a soft, porous, and easily broken and chipped ware. It continues to be a very fragile medium with the color usually some shade of reddish brown.[8]

By the early 1800s, stoneware, to a large extent, had replaced earthenware and red ware. Some of the most elaborately decorated stoneware was made just prior to the Civil War during the 1850s. In the year 1900, government reports show a production of about $1,800,000 worth of stoneware and about $400,000 worth of red ware. The states of Ohio and Pennsylvania led in production. The conservative Pennsylvania Germans made stoneware, but at the same time continued to make their older forms. The development of potteries in the South is difficult to trace even into the 1800s. This kind of industry was not considered important to the economy of the South; thus, few historians have recorded its history. Also, many public records were destroyed during the Civil War.[1]

Pennsylvania, Ohio, and Indiana became the centers of stoneware production. Stoneware is characterized by the glaze used. It is "burned" at a much higher temperature than the previous red ware. The earlier glazes used on red ware would have vaporized or would have been absorbed into the piece if fired at the high temperatures used to make stoneware. Common salt was thrown into the kiln at its highest temperature. The salt would vaporize and deposit itself on the surface of the pottery. It would react with the silica in the clay and form a glassy surface. Sand was sometimes combined with the salt. This process made the surface look like an orange peel in texture. The technique of using salt to glaze pottery was used first in Germany. The process made its way to England and then on to the colonies in the early 1700s. The making of stoneware is virtually the same as red ware, only the glaze and firing are different.[9/1/8]

For the decoration of stoneware, the blue of cobalt salts was almost all that was used since it was not affected by the use of the high temperatures required to fire the pieces. The colors previously used with red ware would not hold up under these high temperatures. The cobalt salts were never applied to a full piece but instead were used to form designs, imprint the potter's trademark and location made, and sometimes a number denoting the content capacity.[1]

Stoneware continued to be made in heavy, utilitarian vessels largely due to the fact that this was the way it had always been produced rather than for necessity. Another kind of pottery was being developed as early as 1830. It was made from a fine clay that was smooth and could be pressed into molds with speed and ease. It was covered with glazes in shades of brown — thus, the name brown ware. The makers in Ohio also called this new product Queensware and Rockingham. The first brown ware was made in a factory production method, a radical departure from methods used to produce stoneware. A company called D. & J. Henderson of Jersey City made some of the first brown ware around 1830. Large quantities were also produced in other areas, such as the Ohio Valley.[9/1]

These were some of the first pieces made using a cast, molded method. Pieces were formed out of plaster of paris molds, allowing production of perfect pieces that showed clearly whatever designs were a part of the mold. Handles were applied separately. Spouts were also applied or "pulled" separately where needed. Pieces were then dried and fired.[1/8]

The unique and one-of-a-kind pieces that had been created on the potter's wheel were replaced with this new technology, allowing for the production of hundreds of pieces from the same mold. Early pieces from a new mold tended to have a stronger, higher relief pattern.

Manufacturers duplicated molds and rarely marked pieces. Even those using a mold for the first time rarely marked their production. This entrepreneurial environment left the door open wide for reproduction of the pieces by other potters. It is, therefore, virtually impossible to identify the maker of most pieces. For example, an incised "star" on the bottom of a piece has been said to be the mark of the Star Stoneware Company, Akron, Ohio. It might also be assumed that most of the pieces having a Dutch theme might have originated in or around the Pennsylvania Dutch country.[1/8]

Many workers were involved in the manufacturing process. One worker might mix the clay, another press the molds, or apply handles and spouts and still another glaze the piece. Firing was also a separate process requiring more workers. The industrialization of pottery in America developed almost 100 years after the same process occurred in England; however, it progressed more quickly here. The rapid movement in America toward industrialization is attributed to the abundance of wood to fire the kilns. In England, firewood was limited and potteries relied on coal to fuel the fires of their kilns.[1/8]

Brown ware was made mostly after 1850 by the same potters who previously had been making red ware and stoneware. Brown ware was "burned" two times. The first firing developed the stoneware evenly and densely followed by the second firing at lower temperatures to set the glaze. Some kilns were also modernized and used coal rather than wood to fire the wares. The rural potteries were very small as evidenced by an 1840 census report in Ohio, referencing 99 Ohio potteries and only 200 workers.[1/8]

Shortly after brown ware, which was commonly called Rockingham, another type of pottery was being made the same way by the same factories but with a clear glaze. This glaze reacted with the clay making a coloration known as yellow ware. The same factories that made brown ware easily made yellow ware as well. Factories in New England and Ohio made the transition easily. After 1845, brown ware and yellow ware were in great production and used everywhere.

Rockingham and yellow ware were made in numerous Ohio cities and towns as well as in Pennsylvania and towns up and down the Mississippi that had river access to move their goods. The bulk of Rockingham and yellow ware is said to have been produced in East Liverpool, Ohio, from 1840 to 1900. East Liverpool grew rapidly, and in 1880 boasted 23 potteries in operation. There were all kinds of combinations of owners and investors such as partnerships, corporations, and individuals who owned and operated potteries.[1/8]

A lot of the wares were sold by peddlers. These door-to-door salesmen for the factories would travel

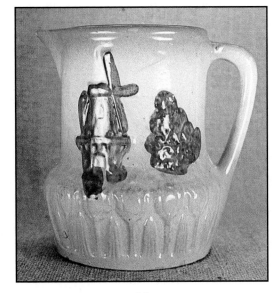

throughout the country until well after 1900 as evidenced by the advent of "advertising" pieces such as promotional rolling pins and other advertising marks sometimes seen on pitchers.

The manufacture of white ware followed next. It was again, like yellow ware, made in the same fashion. White ware is referred to most frequently as hotel ware — a kind of heavy duty china-like ware. Most of the items used in American homes of the time were decorated in colors and almost always imitated. Trenton, New Jersey, emerged as a primary center for true white ware production. Much later, East Liverpool, Ohio, became another large production center.[1/8]

It is also documented that brown ware or Rockingham, Bennington (another famous maker of the period), and yellow ware soon gave way to new glaze colorations including various shades of blue. The major content of this book focuses upon the wares using these new glaze colorations. These new pieces were still molded in factory production with most plants being quite small. Small potters would frequently purchase molds from larger factories and fellow potters who went out of business.[1/8]

Using these new methods, blue accenting which did not fully cover the piece was painted on white backgrounds; however, overall coverage was common with the brown wares. This painting of blue on the piece without full coverage explains the highlighting and diffusing used widely with blue and green.

Transfer prints were also used. The imprint was taken from dampened paper on plates of metal. The wet paper was then evenly pressed on a piece, transferring the image to the

The glass industry expanded greatly and rapidly after the Mason jar caught on. Glass containers began to be used for all sorts of purposes which pottery had previously served. Potters, even the industrialized ones, struggled to find new goods for old markets and found themselves no longer having a market for what had been the majority of their sales, that is food and beverage storage vessels.[8] It can be speculated that the Mason jar invention led to production of many of the pieces seen in this book. As potteries tried to create new goods for their markets, inventiveness in other areas such as tinware and graniteware simultaneously evolved for useful, inexpensive, household necessities.

porous clay surface. Most of these transferred images appear to be blurred. The piece was then dipped in a clear glaze, dried and fired.[1] In addition to transfer prints, sponging was also used as a motif for decorating wares.

In the year 1900, the white ware production of Trenton, New Jersey, and East Liverpool, Ohio, equaled each other. Brown ware, Rockingham, Bennington, and yellow ware were also still being produced.

The screw-top Mason jar as we know it was patented in 1858. The screw-on Mason played an important role in changing all pottery production in America and contributed to the demise of molded utilitarian stoneware use. This jar allowed a new method of food storage, and the industrialized potteries attempted to combat the jar by making a screw-top pottery jar which never caught on. People liked the Mason jar because it was clear.[8]

The invention of the Mason jar was only one of many new ideas that changed the social and home habits of life in America. For years people had let tradition determine what they bought. Now, the new factory production included designers who began to change the traditional shapes and forms. The American public also started to change their buying habits. It was in fashion to have "new" things.[8]

The Pursuit Continues

It is advisable that investment not be the main purpose of collecting stoneware. You must have a passion for it as with any collectible. You have to possess that urge or drive that every time you go antiquing, you just might see that special piece you have been seeking. You must also enjoy living with it, looking at it, decorating with it, and sharing it with friends who can also appreciate its outstanding beauty.

As the search continues, new shapes and patterns will likely surface, allowing the pursuit to continually challenge those having passion for this piece of Americana. Even with the quantity of items shown here, it is certainly not inclusive since not every shape, color, and pattern is included. It is our hope that this book brings the hours of joy to collectors which our predecessors' books have brought to us.

Kathryn McNerney's 1981 book entitled *Blue and White Stoneware* has been an especially invaluable reference and an inspiration to us in our early years of collecting molded stoneware, or salt glaze as it is commonly called. We have carried it to flea markets, shops, and auctions, kept it in the car, and referred to it fervently when information was needed about a piece. For her efforts and those of others, we are grateful. It is our hope that this book will serve as a similar inspiration for new generations of enthusiasts.

American Pottery/Ceramics Classifications

I. Earthenware (opaque). Earthenware production began about 1640 and continued to the end of the colonial period about 1781.

   A. Red ware — considered the first earthenware. It was made from the red clay abundant in America and was a common pottery.

   B. Stoneware — production began in the early 1700s and continued until about 1880.

   C. Molded wares (also known as utility wares)

      1. Brown wares — characterized by glazes in shades of brown, 1830 until after 1900.

         a. American Rockingham — began 1833 with David Henderson and the American Pottery Manufacturing Company from New Jersey. A famous brown ware.

         b. Bennington — begun 1795 by John Norton and Christopher Fenton in Bennington, Vermont, also a famous brown ware.

         c. Yellow ware — made shortly after the beginning of brown ware.

         d. White ware — began late 1800s.

      2. Decorative wares

         a. Artware (art pottery)
         b. Studioware

II. Porcelain (translucent)

   A. China
   B. Parian wares
   C. Belleek wares

Section I – Pitchers

Pitchers were produced in all shapes, sizes, patterns, and colors for purposes of holding and serving mainstay beverages such as milk, buttermilk, and water or a real summer treat, lemonade. Since pitchers received hard usage on a daily basis, cracks and chips are common. Most pitchers were quite heavy on their own, and when filled with liquid, their weight could have easily attributed to the damage often found. Try serving from one of these utilitarian pieces filled with iced tea today; not only will nostalgia prevail, but also biceps will develop from the lifting.

Because of their size, pitchers' pattern markings and mold seams can be seen more clearly than those on most other wares. These pieces were produced in two-part molds. After the two parts were joined to form the whole, seams on the sides received varying degrees of attention. Molds were sometimes designed to camouflage the seams; yet, some roughness needed scraping and smoothing. Thus, side seams are often quite obvious. Handles were usually molded separately and then applied to the molded clay form prior to firing. To attach a handle, criss-cross marks were made on both the body of the pitcher and the ends of the handle with a sharp tool, such as a point of a nail. Water was then added and the two pieces matched with moderate pressure. Additional clay was often added around the joints for strength. Due to the precarious way handles were applied, it is suggested that any older or more fragile piece with a handle receive support under its body when lifting.

Before purchasing a pitcher, the handle should be carefully checked for cracks and repairs. Broken handles are easily glued back and sometimes hardly noticeable. Broken or fractured handles would, of course, reduce the value of a piece.

Since so many pitcher shapes, forms, and colors were produced with such varied and beautiful detail, they continue to be the favorite type of molded stoneware for many collectors.

Acorns

SIZE: 7½"h, 6½"w
AVAILABILITY: Scarce
COLORS: Blue and white only
MINT VALUE: $150.00 – $200.00

A cluster of stenciled acorns and oak leaves gracefully adorns one side only of this smaller pitcher. The applied handle with built-in thumb grip securely joins the collar of the pitcher. Molded scrolling decorates the collar between the handle and pulled lip on each side. The slightly bulbous body is typically accentuated with light blue diffusing around the top and bottom. The example shown has a hairline fracture in the handle which slightly reduces its condition rating and value.

American Beauty Rose

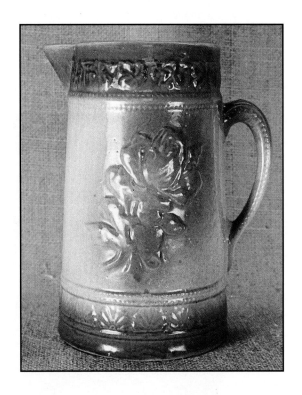

The American Beauty Rose pitcher features large open roses on a smooth background. Open fan-like moldings encircle the bottom of the pitcher below a double beaded row. The top detail features flower petals above double beading. Diffused blue highlights the centered rose as well as the top and bottom rims. The centered applied handle is also beaded. The two examples above illustrate varying shades of blue diffusing.

SIZE: 10"h, 7"w
AVAILABILITY: Rare pattern
COLORS: Blue and white, spongeware
MINT VALUE: $400.00 – $500.00

While difficult to capture in a photo, this American Beauty Rose pitcher with dark blue sponging is an extremely rare addition to any collection. All features are the same as the examples above. Because of its rarity, a spongeware example in this pattern can easily be valued in the $800.00 – $1,000.00 range.

∽———Apricot———∾

SIZE: 8"h, 5"w
AVAILABILITY: Common pattern
COLORS: Blue and white only
MINT VALUE: $250.00 – $350.00

An Apricot pitcher is shown at left with its companion butter crock in the same pattern. The Apricot with honeycomb pattern was also used on salt holders, butter crocks, and bowls. While the green and cream colors were commonly used for butters and bowls, various shades of blue and white appear to be the primary colors for pitchers.

Of all pitchers, the Apricot is one of the most commonly seen. Each of the three pitchers shown has excellent deep molding and slightly different coloration with the example shown above left having very dark blue coloring. Being a common pattern, wide variations from light to dark blue coloration can be found. The cluster of apricots and leaves is framed by a medallion of scrolling and intricate molding on a honeycomb background. The applied handle is roped. Good mold patterns will show the veins on the leaves.

Avenue of Trees

SIZES: 9"h, 7"w
8"h, 7¾"w
7"h, 7½"w
6"h, 5½"w
5"h, 4½"w
4"h, 3¾"w
AVAILABILITY: Rare pattern
COLORS: Blue and white, solid blue, solid green, solid brown
MINT VALUE: Varies according to size and color (values chart provided on next page)

The Avenue of Trees series is available in many sizes, from small creamers to large buttermilk pitchers, and in several colors including desirable blue and white as well as solid blue, green, and brown glazes. The pattern is the same on both sides with graceful Doric columns providing the frame for a three-dimensional effect of trees lining a lane which leads to a gate at its end. Note the wheel tracks on the lane. A rolled-in top rim and matching bottom are uniquely characteristic to the Avenue of Trees pattern. Color and size comparisons are shown below for 9", 6", and 4" examples.

Blue and white examples typically have pale coloring with diffusing around the top and bottom. Blue and white 8" and 7" examples are shown at left. Note the slightly different bottom rim treatment for the smaller pitcher.

Sample values for several sizes and colors of the Avenue of Trees pitcher series:

	Blue and White	Solid Blue	Green	Brown
9" x 7"	$250.00 – $300.00	$200.00 – $250.00	$100.00 – $150.00	$75.00 – $125.00
6" x 5½"	$200.00 – $250.00	$150.00 – $200.00	$95.00 – $125.00	$65.00 – $100.00
4" x 3¾"	$175.00 – $200.00	$125.00 – $150.00	$65.00 – $100.00	$50.00 – $100.00

Mint values for patterns with such an array of sizes and colors are quite difficult to pinpoint. Larger blue and white examples typically command the higher prices; however, smaller sizes are often more rare and can command larger prices also.

Because of hard, everyday usage, molded stoneware often fell victim to being chipped and broken. Pieces should be examined carefully for possible repair as illustrated around the rim of this Avenue of Trees pitcher. While personal taste and preference of the collector dictate the acceptability of repairs, sellers should clearly indicate when repairs have been made. Slight differences in stoneware color and glaze color, seen around the top and inside rim above, can be detected upon close examination.

Basketweave and Morning Glory

SIZE: 9"h, 5¼"w
AVAILABILITY: Scarce
COLORS: Blue and white, solid green, yellow
MINT VALUES: Blue and white: $250.00 – $300.00
Solid green: $200.00 – $250.00
Yellow: $175.00 – $225.00
Mugs: $75.00 – $125.00 each

An entire house could have been outfitted using the Basketweave and Morning Glory pattern. Kitchenwares as well as washstand sets were produced in this popular pattern which features an upwardly sweeping stem of morning glories on a basketweave background. Both sides have the same pattern. The square-top applied handle is roped. The pitcher is tall and narrow with slight tapering to the top and was produced in blue and white, yellow, and solid green versions. As seen below, a Basketweave and Morning Glory pitcher with matching mugs is an impressive set.

∾————**Bluebirds**————∿

SIZE: 9"h, 7"w
AVAILABILITY: Extremely rare pattern
COLORS: Blue and white
MINT VALUE: $450.00 – $550.00

Three flying bluebirds are featured sweeping downward toward the bottom of the handle on each side of this heavy pitcher. Dark blue highlighting on the birds as well as on the bands around the top and bottom provides sharp contrast with the glazed white clay. The applied handle has a spur for easy gripping, and the large lip accents the pitcher's unique form.

∾————**Butterfly**————∿

SIZE: 10"h, 5"w
AVAILABILITY: Scarce
COLORS: Blue and white
MINT VALUE: $350.00 – $500.00

Heavy orange peel texturing provides the background for the large butterfly in the medallion at center which is surrounded by raised roping. Highlighted by dark blue diffusing, rings of smaller butterflies between raised roping surround the top and bottom. The roping theme is continued in the style of the applied handle.

Wide variations in coloring and pattern clarity are typical with molded stoneware as is evidenced by the three examples of the Butterfly pitcher shown. This pattern is notorious for having faint mold markings.

Castle (or Monastery and Fishscale)

While used predominantly on washstand pieces, the fishscale background is uniquely used on this Castle pattern table pitcher. Its pattern is also often referred to as Monastery and Fishscale.

SIZES: Small pitcher: 8¼"h, 5½"w
Large pitcher: 9"h, 7½"w
Creamer: 5"h, 5"w
AVAILABILITY: Common for pitcher, rare for creamer
COLORS: Blue and white, solid blue, brown
MINT VALUES: Pitcher: Blue and white: $175.00 – $250.00
Brown: $95.00 – $125.00
Creamer: Solid blue: $100.00 – $150.00

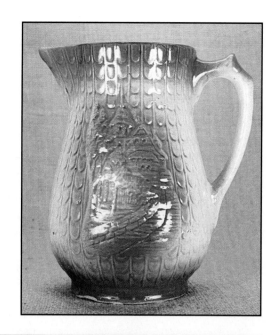

The castle features three turreted roofs atop a mountain with a long, winding brick drive. Larger and smaller versions of the pitcher were produced along with a creamer. The bulbous bottom gracefully tapers inward toward the top which has a well-defined spout. The applied handle has a slight thumb spur. While blue and white as well as brown colors were used on the pitchers, the creamer is most frequently seen in solid blue.

⌒— Cattail —⌒

SIZE: 7"h, 5"w
AVAILABILITY: Rare pattern
COLORS: Blue and white
MINT VALUE: $175.00 – $250.00

A single, dark blue, stenciled cattail appears on only one side of this smaller pitcher. The handle is accented with a brushing of blue while blue bands encircle the top rim and base. A pattern of scrolling is embossed around the collar. Notice the generous amount of clay used to attach the bottom of the handle.

Cattails and Rushes

SIZES: Large: 10"h, 5½"w
Medium: 9½"h, 5"w
Small: 7½"h, 4½"w
Mug: 4½"h, 3"w
AVAILABILITY: Rare pattern
COLORS: Blue and white
MINT VALUES: Large: $300.00 – $350.00
Medium: $275.00 – $300.00
Small: $250.00 – $300.00
Mug: $175.00 – $200.00
With advertising, add $100.00

Masses of cattails and rushes create a splash on the body of this very simply formed pitcher. Molded bands around the top and bottom provide the only other accenting.

Two sizes of the Cattails and Rushes pitcher are shown above, along with a quite rare mug in the same pattern.

The color highlighting of the large pitcher above, right, is especially rare with vertical stripes of blue similar to a swirling effect. An example like this would command a higher price. The side view (facing page) shows a band of vertical striping which incorporates the unusually wide handle. The smaller pitcher has a slightly bulbous bottom and a squared handle style as compared to the larger size. The smaller Cattails and Rushes pitcher at left shows the more typical coloration used.

An extremely rare Cattails and Rushes pitcher with advertising is presented at left. Notice that the spout is distinctly molded rather than gently curved from the pitcher's body.

Cherry Cluster

SIZE: 8"h, 5½"w (bottom)
AVAILABILITY: Rare pattern
COLORS: Blue and white, brown
MINT VALUE: Blue and white: $650.00 – $700.00
Brown: $125.00 – 175.00

Makers must have reserved this pitcher form for some of their most beautiful patterns, including the Flying Birds in addition to this elegant Cherry Cluster pattern.

With a flared lip and bottom, tapered body, and graceful handle with pinky grip, the style accents the large cluster of cherries and leaves presented on the overall waffle background. The top and bottom are accented by a wreath of delicate cherry leaves. This pattern is sometimes referred to as Dainty Fruit. While predominantly produced in blue and white, it is also found in brown.

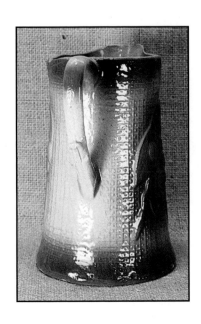

Cherry Cluster and Basketweave

SIZES: Large: 9"h, 6"w (bottom)
Small: 6½"h, 4½"w (bottom)
AVAILABILITY: Rare pattern
COLORS: Blue and white
MINT VALUES: Large: $350.00 – $375.00
Small: $275.00 – $300.00

    The same cluster of cherries and leaves as is on the Cherry Cluster pitcher is presented on this Cherry Cluster on Basketweave pattern. In large and small sizes, the basketweave background is used with roping on the applied handle. The pattern is the same on both sides.

Cherries and Leaves

SIZES: Large: 9¼"h, 5"w (bottom)
Small: 8½"h, 4½"w (bottom)
AVAILABILITY: Rare pattern
COLORS: Blue and white
MINT VALUES: $300.00 – $350.00
$375.00 – $450.00 with advertising

With very plain styling, this pitcher is accented with an elegant molded band of cherries and leaves around the top and bottom. The embossed bands are consistently highlighted in very pale blue with the mid-section remaining white. The applied handle has a squared grip at the top, and the pouring spout is a gracefully flared, well-defined part of the mold.

Produced by the Red Wing Union Stoneware Company of Red Wing, Minnesota (1906 – 1930), the pitcher was very popular for advertising because of the large plain white area on its sides. Several promotional examples are shown on this page — one from Iowa (Moore Bros.), and one from Wisconsin (L. H. Meysembourg). The small version bearing the message "MERRY CHRISTMAS/ANDRES WESTIN & CO." is an extremely unique example. The mold pattern is somewhat faint.

Columns and Arches

SIZE: 8¾"h, 5"w (bottom)
AVAILABILITY: Rare pattern
COLORS: Blue and white
MINT VALUE: $425.00 – $550.00

The Columns and Arches pitcher is one of the most graceful, elegant, and detailed produced. With mold patterns over its entire surface, it could almost be compared to a work of ancient Greek art.

Graceful columns bearing Ionic capitals support brick arches on a brick background. The handle has an unusual mortise and tenon detailing at the top and is accented with beading in a trough along its sides. The slightly flared top is accented by still another pattern of diagonal lattice. Variation in hue is typical as is evidenced by the examples shown.

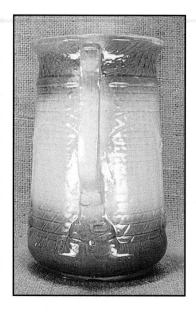

Daisy Cluster

SIZE: 7"h, 7"w
AVAILABILITY: Extremely rare pattern
COLORS: Blue and white
MINT VALUE: $600.00 – $725.00

As an extremely rare and beautifully detailed pitcher, two examples of coloration are shown for this Daisy Cluster pitcher. A cluster of large daisies and leaves is centered on each side while panels of diagonal lattice with scrolled borders are draped over the lip and handle. The bulbous body is topped with a narrow collar which is accented with a symmetrical band of horizontal tulips from lip to handle on each side.

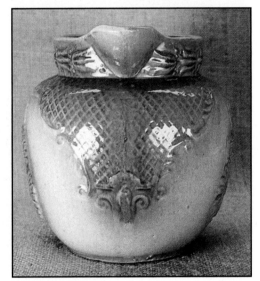

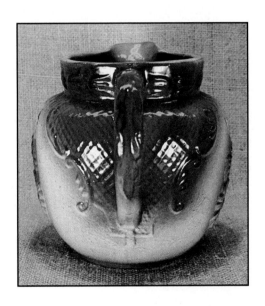

Doe and Fawn

SIZE: 8½"h 6"w
AVAILABILITY: Common
COLORS: Blue and white, solid blue
MINT VALUE: $175.00 – $225.00

Flora and fauna provided the imagery for most molded stoneware patterns with deer getting their share of attention on this Doe and Fawn pitcher as well as the Leaping Deer and Stag and Pine Tree patterns. The slightly bulbous bottom is accented by a strong mold pattern featuring a doe standing by her fawn under a large tree. The simple handle could have been part of the mold rather than applied.

The example below right shows a couple of "pits" on and just below the doe. "Pits" occurred when air bubbles were trapped as the clay was pressed into the molds. The air bubbles later burst during or after the firing and glazing process. With respect to value, "pits" are, of course, not desirable but should not be considered as detrimental as chips or fractures. Collectors must keep in mind that molded stoneware was produced inexpensively for common, everyday use.

The left example does have a small chip on the pouring spout which would reduce its condition to Good and thus affect its value according to pricing criteria.

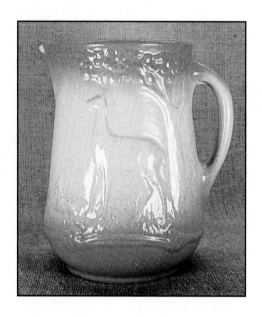 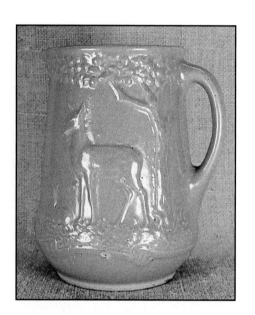

Dutch Children and Windmill

SIZE: 7½"h, 6"w
AVAILABILITY: Common pattern
COLORS: Blue and white, blue and green
MINT VALUE: $175.00 – $225.00

The Dutch Children and Windmill pattern is the most commonly available pitcher in the Dutch series which includes several uniquely shaped pitchers. An embossed Dutch boy and girl appear to be kissing with a windmill in the background. Both sides bear the same pattern. The embossed figures are each highlighted in dark blue on the example below with lighter blue diffused bands around the top and bottom of the pitcher. A band of embossed tulips surrounds the base with another band of flowers just above it. (See facing page, top right.)

The example above has a unique and rare half-blue, half-green color scheme. Most pitchers in this pattern are available in the blue and white coloring. Another coloring motif features the boy and girl highlighted in light brown with blue diffusing around the top and bottom.

The close-up at right shows how handles can be quite fragile. Notice the separation crack at the bottom attachment. Even with a generous amount of clay used to attach the handle, the firing process, as well as time, can take its toll.

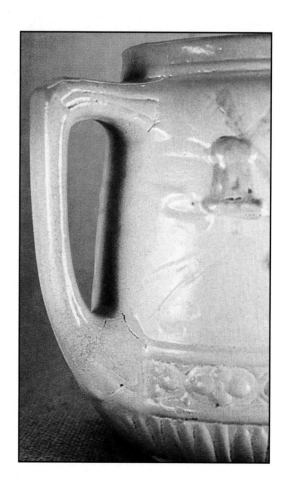

Dutch Farm Scene

SIZE: 7½"h, 6½"w
AVAILABILITY: Scarce pattern
COLORS: Blue and white
MINT VALUE: $175.00 – $225.00

A dark blue stenciled scene of two Dutch children and their dog with a windmill and barn in the background appears on only one side of this pitcher which is surrounded at the top and bottom by large, fully opened blossoms. The opposite side of the pitcher at right clearly shows the flower detailing. The blue diffusing around the top and bottom is characteristically pale as on most examples found.

Dutch Landscape Scene

SIZE: 9"h, 5¼"w (bottom)
AVAILABILITY: Common pattern
COLORS: Blue and white
MINT VALUE: $150.00 – $200.00

The Dutch boy and girl pattern is stenciled in blue on this Dutch Landscape pitcher. This very plain pitcher is dressed up with the stenciled scene on both sides as well as bands of diffused blue around the top and bottom.

Banded Dutch Landscape Scene

SIZE: 9"h, 5¼"w (bottom)
AVAILABILITY: Scarce pattern
COLORS: Blue and white
MINT VALUE: $150.00 – $200.00

The Dutch boy and girl pattern is stenciled in blue on this Dutch Landscape pitcher. This plain white pitcher is embellished with the stenciled scene on both sides and bands of dark blue around the top rim (as shown below) and around the bottom. This is the same stenciling as used on the example on the facing page as well as on several other wares including an extremely rare Dutch rolling pin which is shown in that separate section.

The seam line below the handle on the side is noticeable at right. Some makers were more careful than others about smoothing the clay where the two parts of the mold were joined.

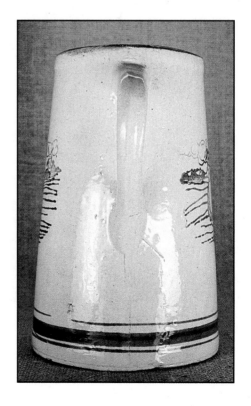

——Dutch Windmill and Bush——

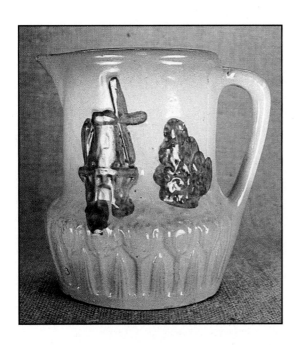

SIZE: 7"h, 5½"w
AVAILABILITY: Common pattern
COLORS: Blue and white
MINT VALUE: $225.00 – $275.00

The Dutch Windmill and Bush pattern is another of the unique small shapes in the Dutch series. Straight sides flare at the base as if providing room for the surrounding row of tulips in full bloom. The embossed windmill and bush are both highlighted in deep blue; lighter blue diffusing accents the pitcher's top and bottom. The handle treatment is somewhat unusual in that it extends almost vertically from the base and curves in for the top attachment. The same scene appears on both sides.

——Dutch Windmill and Sailboat——

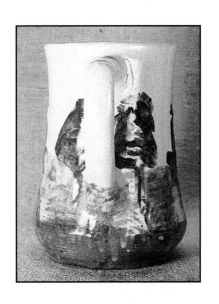

SIZE: 7½"h, 4½"w
AVAILABILITY: Scarce pattern
COLORS: Blue and white
MINT VALUE: $225.00 – $275.00

On each side a large embossed windmill perches by the sea as boats with billowing sails chart their courses (near handle). The windmill and sails are highlighted in dark blue while application of much blue around the base creates the "sea."

∽——— Eagle ———∽

The Eagle pitcher uses roping decoration and a distinctive background of impressed dots to highlight the majestic eagle at center. The large medallion is repeated on both sides with the eagle in flight clutching a shield and arrows. As one of the most desirable molded stoneware pitchers, the eagle is intricately detailed with extensive roping and scrolling. The dark blue coloring and deep molding enhance the mint value of this example.

Eagle, continued . . .

SIZES:　　　Large: 8"h, 5"w
　　　　　　　Small: 7"h, 4"w
AVAILABILITY:　Extremely rare pattern, small size extremely rare
COLORS:　　Blue and white only
MINT VALUES:　Large: $600.00 – $800.00
　　　　　　　Small: $1,200.00 – $1,500.00

The seven-inch tall Eagle pitcher at right is considered one of the rarest pieces which may be included in any collection. The same pitcher is seen in front of the pitcher grouping in the top photo for size comparison.

Although cobalt oxide was considered to be more reliable in color consistency under high temperature firing, this collection of wares bearing the Eagle pattern has distinctively different shades of blue. The grouping in the center photo consists of the salt holder at left, pitcher at center, and butter holder at right. The average mint value for these three pieces would amount to approximately $1,975.00.

Flying Birds

SIZE: 8¼"h, 5"w (bottom)
AVAILABILITY: Rare pattern
COLORS: Blue and white, green and brown
MINT VALUES: $500.00 – $550.00 (blue and white)
$250.00 – $300.00 (green and brown)
Mugs: $175.00 – $200.00

This Flying Birds pitcher has the uncommon characteristic of different patterns on each side. The Lovebirds pattern is presented on one side while the Flying Birds pattern can be found on the opposite side. The same pattern scheme prevails on the salt holder, grease jar, bowls, and cookie jar.

The Flying Birds pitcher makes an absolutely stunning set when combined with a color-matched set of Flying Birds mugs.

Since most people would lift the pitcher with their right hand, the front side of the pitcher features a pair of birds perched on a twig adorned with flowers and leaves. Notice that a bird in flight is to the upper left and upper right — a feature which is not included on other wares using this pattern. The opposite, or back side, features the loving pair in flight with their friends from the front side just above them. The bottom and top are banded with rows of small flowers. The handle is beaded and has a petite pinky spur toward its bottom. The pitcher gracefully sweeps inward and upward from a base which is larger than the body and has a well-defined spout for easy pouring.

The green and brown two-tone coloration on the example above is quite unusual particularly with the extremely clear mold markings.

⁓———— Girl and Dog————⁓

Framed in a simple oval on each side, the dog sits on his haunches awaiting a treat from his master who is kneeling. Accented with simple mold bands around the top and bottom, the Girl and Dog pitcher characteristically has generous pale blue highlighting. The mold pattern is notoriously very faint and almost indiscernible on most examples seen.

SIZE: 9"h, 5½"w (bottom)
AVAILABILITY: Extremely rare pattern
COLORS: Blue and white, spongeware
MINT VALUES: Blue and white: $650.00 – $700.00
Spongeware: $800.00 – $1,200.00

While most sponging was used to accent very plain wares, makers occasionally dared to be different by sponging a patterned piece as was done with the Girl and Dog pitcher at right. While impossible to capture fully in a photograph, the oval band can be seen. A sponged example like this is one degree beyond extremely rare.

Grape Cluster on Basketweave

While other grape patterns are more commonly seen, this Grape Cluster on Basketweave is unusual. The grapes pattern, being the same as that seen on the Grape Cluster with Rickrack pattern, clings to a tight basketweave background which is different from the typical basketweave pattern used. The top and bottom are accented with a wide band of rickrack.

SIZE:	8"h, 5"w
AVAILABILITY:	Rare pattern
COLORS:	Blue and white
MINT VALUE:	$300.00 – $350.00

Light, almost slate blue diffusing splashes over the grape cluster area on each side as well as around the top and bottom. The seam on the side is quite obvious but was cleaned and smoothed by the maker quite nicely, and the pulled lip is well formed.

Grape Cluster with Rickrack

As the focal point for the Grape Cluster with Rickrack pitcher, the large center cluster of grapes seems to almost hang from the waffle background as if in a vineyard ripe for harvest. The larger base tapers slightly to a smaller top rim with both the base and rim accented with bands of rickrack. With the rickrack fading on an upward leg on each side, the waffle background pattern is continued over the pouring lip.

Grape Cluster with Rickrack, continued . . .

SIZES:	Small: 6¾"h, 4"w (bottom)
	Medium: 8"h, 5½"w (bottom)
	Large: 9½"h, 5½"w (bottom)
AVAILABILITY:	Common
COLORS:	Blue and white, solid blue, blue and tan, brown, solid green, spongeware
MINT VALUES:	$200.00 – $250.00 (blue and white, blue and tan)
	$300.00 – 350.00 (blue and white spongeware)
	$125.00 – $175.00 (solid green)
	$75.00 – $100.00 (brown)
	(smaller sizes valued the same since they are actually more scarce)

Wide variations in color are seen as is evidenced by these blue and white examples. Slight differences in patterns may be seen even on examples which may have been marked on the bottom by the same maker. Comparing the green and blue examples, notice that the bottom of the green grape cluster curves to the right, whereas the bottom of the blue grape cluster curves to the left. More grapevine stems are seen above the green grape cluster than above the blue grape cluster, and the small cluster of grapes on the green pitcher is farther down and to the right than it is on the blue pitcher. The maker of the molds may be accountable for these slight differences rather than the maker of the pitchers. One mold maker may have produced a very similar but slightly different pattern so as not to infringe upon the design of another mold maker.

Produced in several sizes and a variety of colors including rarely seen spongeware, Grape Cluster with Rickrack pitchers typically have very clear mold markings; occasionally one will be seen with a faint pattern. A star molded on the bottom center of one of these pitchers indicates the mark of its maker, the Northstar Stoneware Company of Red Wing, Minnesota.

Although an example is not shown, a very similar pattern with a band of leaves around the top instead of rickrack is known as Grape Cluster with Leaf Band and was produced by the Uhl Pottery Company, Huntingburg, Indiana. Mugs were also produced in the Grape Cluster with Leaf Band pattern.

Grape Cluster on Trellis

SIZES: Large: 9½"h, 6"w (bottom)
             Medium: 8½"h, 5"w (bottom)
             Small: 7"h, 4" (bottom)
             Creamer: 5"h, 4"w (bottom)
             Squat pitcher: 5½"h, 7"w (bottom); 6½"h
                with lid
AVAILABILITY: Rare pattern and sizes
COLORS: Blue and white, solid blue (dark, medium,
                light), blue and tan
MINT VALUES: Pitchers: $225.00 – $275.00 each

The Grape Cluster on Trellis pitchers were produced in a variety of sizes, shapes, and colors. Three tall pitchers and a smaller creamer with slanting sides, shown here in blue and white, dark blue, and light blue colorings, as well as a squat pitcher with lid were produced. This pitcher has a similar pattern of grapes, leaves, and vines as seen on the Grape Cluster on Basketweave, Grape Cluster with Rickrack and Grape Cluster with Leaf Band patterns. The upright pitcher form at bottom right features a large cluster of grapes on each side flanked by a large leaf on each side with connecting vines. The pattern has an open trellis background accented with a band of grape leaves around the top and bottom.

The shorter, squat styles actually show two different patterns on the trellis background. The blue and white version at top and the solid dark blue one at center have a slightly different pattern from the one at bottom left. As with the pattern differences for the Grape Cluster with Rickrack pattern, the maker of the molds may be accountable for these slight differences. Pitcher makers may have also produced slightly different patterns for the same reason.

These shorter versions usually had a lid with a knob which was shaped to extend over the very pointed lip. Unfortunately, the lids are missing from each of the examples shown.

Grape Cluster in Shield

A cluster of grapes, leaves, and vine in a shield appears on each side of these pitchers. A band of ribbing around the top and bottom accented by rows of overlapping leaves and beading provides a frame for an almost bark-like background. Pitchers in at least four sizes as well as matching mugs were produced in a variety of colors including green and cream, yellow, blue and white, brown, and several shades of solid green. Examples in blue and white coloring are rarely seen. Size comparison groupings are shown above. A mug is shown below.

SIZES: Small: 7"h, 4¼"w (bottom)
              Medium: 8¼"h, 5"w (bottom)
              Large: 8¾"h, 5½"w (bottom)
              Extra Large: 9¾"h, 6½"w (bottom)
              Mug: 4¾"h, 3½"w (bottom)
AVAILABILITY: Common
COLORS: Blue and white, blue and tan, brown,
              green and cream, solid green, yellow
MINT VALUES: Small: $150.00 – $200.00
              Medium: $125.00 – $150.00
              Large: $250.00 – $275.00
              Extra Large: $275.00 – $325.00
              Mug: $50.00 – $75.00
              (for solid green and brown examples,
              deduct 40 percent)

Grape Cluster in Shield, continued . . .

This very large Grape Cluster in Shield pitcher has excellent, deep coloration and mold markings. (This is the now-famous "first piece" ever purchased by Terry and Kay Lowrance and the one upon which the "pursuit" was begun by both the Lowrances and Terry Taylor.)

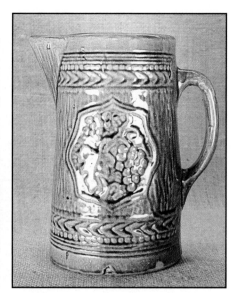

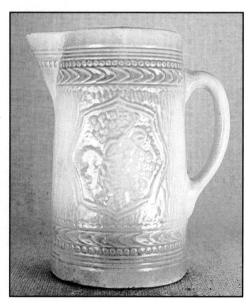

Solid green examples in the Grape Cluster in Shield pattern are quite commonly seen with green and cream and brown examples less frequently available. Yellow as well as blue and white examples are rarely seen. Brown and yellow pieces typically have white glazed interiors.

Grazing Cows

Grazing Cows pitchers in any color are a beautiful tribute to the utilitarian purposes of molded stoneware. Even with the purpose of many molded stoneware items having a relationship with the products and by-products of cows (milk, buttermilk, butter, etc.), few pattern designs featured them. In addition to this pattern, only the Cows and Fence and the Cows and Columns butter holders use cows as a part of the mold pattern.

SIZES: Small: 6½"h, 4"w (bottom)
Medium: 7½"h, 4½"w (bottom)
Large: 8"h, 5"w (bottom)
AVAILABILITY: Large size, common; other sizes, extremely rare
Yellow, extremely rare color
COLORS: Blue and white, green and cream, yellow, brown
MINT VALUES: Small: $500.00 – $600.00
Medium: $400.00 – $500.00
Large: $250.00 – $300.00
(for brown, deduct 50 percent)

Commonly seen in blue and white, green and cream, and brown, the Grazing Cows pattern was also produced in a rarely seen yellow. Brown and yellow examples have white glazed interiors. The eight-inch size is commonly seen while other sizes are considered extremely rare in any color.

Whether a creative effort on the part of the maker, an experiment, or limited purposeful production, two-tone pitchers such as the green and brown example above are occasionally seen.

Examples with dark blue coloration are quite desirable with smaller dark blue and white examples typically commanding premium prices. Blue and white examples can be found in hues ranging from quite light to very deep. While only three sizes are presented, a size larger and a size smaller than those shown were produced.

At first glance the dark blue and white Grazing Cows pitcher below left looks like a wonderful example. Closer inspection reveals major repairs have been made to the bottom and top rim. At right, notice that a patch of clay has been added inside. Below right notice that the mold pattern near the pitcher's bottom has been lost with the addition of clay to fill a chipped area. In fact, the entire bottom was severed, and the repair included gluing, patching, and painting. The color match is quite good and is better captured by photography than can even be seen by the naked eye. Many collectors use black lights as a device for detecting repairs like this one which may not be noted by sellers.

A story was relayed by a collector who told a seller that he always placed newly purchased pieces of molded stoneware in the dishwasher as a means of thorough cleaning. The seller gasped at the dishwasher idea, saying it would damage these types of wares. The collector nonetheless placed the piece in the dishwasher as usual and discovered that the paint applied to the repaired areas was washed off along with the dust and dirt!

Most sellers are reputable and do not try to camouflage repaired pieces; yet, inspections need to be carefully done prior to paying mint values. The acceptability of damages and/or repairs is entirely up to the collector. Commonly referred to as "shelf pieces," examples with some damage can be used for display with the damaged part turned to the back of the shelf. Examples in less than mint condition also often carry greatly reduced prices. The condition of a piece is typically not as critical for "shelf pieces" as it may be for investment or resale purposes.

Because it is commonly available, the Grazing Cows pitcher is often a first purchase for a molded stoneware collection. The mold pattern over the entire exterior features a pair of grazing cows centered on each side in a medallion framed by beading and roping. Very clear mold patterns will show even the horns on the cows. The impressed dots background is accented at the top and bottom by bands of intricate scrolls and roping. The applied handle also has an intricately roped pattern. Notice that the scrolling and roping pattern extends around the lip at the top.

Indian in War Bonnet

An Indian in full head dress is centered in a simply framed medallion. The clear, deep molding of these examples distinctly shows the waffle pattern of the background. The simple rounded band which frames the Indian is repeated with a double row around the top and bottom. The Indian is typically highlighted in diffused color with additional diffused bands of color around the top and bottom. The applied handle is roped with a slight thumb grip at the top.

SIZE: 8¼"h, 5¼"w
AVAILABILITY: Rare pattern
COLORS: Blue and white, green and cream (extremely rare)
MINT VALUE: $350.00 – $450.00

Several examples of the Indian in War Bonnet pitcher are presented with different coloration. The typical blue coloring seen on the pitchers at top has a slight slate hue. Notice that the coloration of the example at bottom left has a speckled effect. The use of color on handles typically varied. Examples with green and cream color are quite rare and could command a higher price.

Indian in War Bonnet (Reproduction)

It is hopefully obvious that this example of the Indian in War Bonnet pitcher is a reproduction. Its purpose for inclusion here is to aid the collector in recognizing reproductions. Only a limited number of items has been reproduced; nevertheless, many beginning collectors are often tempted by the mint condition and possibly lower price. The Indian in War Bonnet pattern along with Grazing Cows, Eagle, Lovebirds, and Sleepy Eye are the pitchers most typically seen in reproductions.

The blue coloring on reproductions is typically consistent, whereas coloring found on original pieces varies widely. As well, the hue is generally darker on newer pieces. The glaze on reproduction pieces is typically very shiny and lacks the "patina" of an older example. Typically, the most notable characteristic of a reproduction is in the interior as can be seen at right. Enough clay was pressed into molds for original pieces so that the interior had no indentations where parts of the pattern protruded on the outside. Interior indentations can be easily seen on this reproduction example. Old molds are, of course, often used for what are being called reproductions.

Another avenue, although not foolproof, for detecting reproduction pieces is to "thump" its side as if thumping a piece of crystal. Older pieces, particularly those showing any wear, will respond with a thud; new ware will typically ring almost like a piece of crystal. However, keep in mind that some old examples can be found in truly mint condition; their reaction to a "thump" may also be a ring but typically not to the extent of a reproduction.

Finally, beware of dirt. If a piece is dirty, the dirt should "look old," not new. Reputable sellers will certainly make no representation that these reproductions are old; yet, there are some who will price them according to old examples and even bury them in dirt to advance the aging process.

～ ——Indian Boy and Girl—— ～

SIZE: 6½"h, 5"w (bottom)
AVAILABILITY: Scarce pattern
COLORS: Blue and white, brown
MINT VALUES: Blue and white: $300.00 – $350.00
Brown: $125.00 – $150.00

This small pitcher is also referred to by the title Captain John Smith and Pocahontas as well as Kissing Pilgrims, depending on locale and individual preference. The figures on each side are framed by a wreath of daisies. The top and bottom rims are accented with a large beaded band and broken line. The applied handle has a log pattern as if carrying out the frontier theme of the pattern.

Kathryn McNerney, in her book titled *Blue & White Stoneware* (1981), provided such an excellent description for this pitcher that it is quite worthy of repeating in paraphrased form. Stories relate that once Captain John Smith and Pocahontas were married, he liked to see his wife dressed in the manner she appears on the pitcher. He bought many of her dresses himself selecting English schoolgirl types with big sashes and sailor collars. Her headdress remains in place even with her English schoolgirl attire. The Captain (or gentleman) appears to be dressed in a waist coat and top hat typical of the period. On one side of the pitcher the couple stands apart as though in conversation. On the other side he is closely looking into her face and gently stroking her chin with his right hand.

Iris

The tall, slender style of the Iris pitcher provides an elegant setting for the single iris stem which is flanked on each side by a sword-shaped leaf. From its mid-section, the pitcher gently flares outward toward its top and its bottom which is accented with a wide band of vertical ribbing. A star pattern which resembles tufting encircles the pitcher's top. The gracefully curved handle has a thumb-grip spur on top.

SIZE: 8½"h, 4½"w (bottom)
AVAILABILITY: Rare pattern
COLORS: Blue and white, multicolored
MINT VALUE: Blue and white: $350.00 – $400.00
Multicolored: $175.00 – 225.00

The iris and leaves mold pattern is typically highlighted in dark blue with bands of lighter blue around the top and base. The example at right is uniquely highlighted with dark blue bands at top and bottom. Labeled as "Early Roseville pottery," the example shown at left is more colorfully accented.

Leaping Deer

SIZE: 8"h, 5½"w (bottom)
AVAILABILITY: Scarce
COLORS: Blue and white, brown, spongeware
MINT VALUES: Blue and white: $350.00 – $400.00
Spongeware: $1,000.00 – $1,500.00
Brown: $125.00 – $150.00

The intricately designed Leaping Deer pattern features a large center medallion of laurel sprigs, flowers, and ribbons on each side serving as a frame for the agile buck in action. A diamond lattice background is enhanced by a band of harp-style scrolling around the top and onto the lip while the bottom is encircled by a repeating band of laurel sprigs. The applied handle is beaded. The overall design of the Leaping Deer is the same as the Swan pitcher, the only difference being the pattern within the medallion.

Leaping Deer, continued . . .

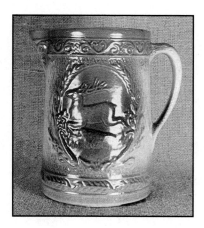

Several examples in blue and white as well as brown are shown here. The top left example has a small chip on its lip which would reduce its value. An extremely rare dark blue sponge on pristine white clay example is shown on the previous page. While not fully captured by photography, the mold pattern is excellent; the sparse sponging is also unique.

Lincoln Head

A bust of the famous president is clearly embossed on each side of the Lincoln Head pitcher series. With a log cabin nestled among trees at the base (see side view) the President admiringly remembers his heritage. The Lincoln Head series was produced in five sizes by the Uhl Pottery Company in Huntingburg, Indiana. Found in a variety of hues, the six-inch tall example shown has diffused blue around the bottom fading to white at the top. The upward tapering form features a large flared lip with the handle having a well-defined thumb grip.

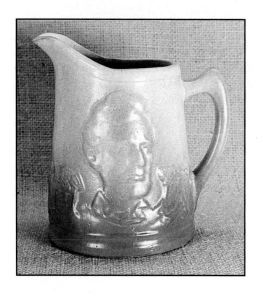

SIZES: 10"h, 7"w
8"h, 6"w
7"h, 5"w
6"h, 4"w
4¾"h, 4¾"w
AVAILABILITY: Extremely rare pattern
COLORS: Blue and white
MINT VALUES: $450.00 – $500.00 each

∽──────Lovebirds──────∽

While most patterns feature detailing which was specific to that pattern, the same overall design is used for the Lovebirds, Eagle, and Grazing Cows pitchers. The only difference among the three pitcher patterns is the content of the centered medallion. An impressed dots background accented with bands of scrolling and roping around the top and bottom allows focus to be placed on the centered medallion on each side. Notice that the scrolling and roping around the top are continued around the lip.

Lovebirds, continued . . .

SIZE: 8"h, 5"w (bottom)
AVAILABILITY: Rare pattern
COLORS: Blue and white, brown, yellow
MINT VALUES: Blue and white: $400.00 – $450.00
Yellow: $500.00 – $600.00
Brown: $150.00 – $200.00

The pair of lovebirds is framed by roping and beading around the medallion. The applied handle also features the roping pattern. The Lovebirds pitcher is most commonly seen in blue and white, occasionally in brown, and very rarely in yellow.

The brown example shown at bottom right has an unglazed spot on one bird. Spots like this were characteristic of brown glazes which gave them a reputation for undependability in firing at high temperatures.

Old Fashioned Garden Rose

The Old Fashioned Garden Rose pattern was a popular one for sponging decoration. Although quite rare and unique, patterns are often indiscernible on spongeware examples. The deep mold pattern of this example, however, allows for both the beauty of the pattern to show as well as the sponging to be appreciated.

Old Fashioned Garden Rose, continued . . .

SIZE: 9"h, 5"w (bottom)
AVAILABILITY: Extremely rare pattern
COLORS: Blue and white, sponge
MINT VALUES: Blue and white: $450.00 – $500.00
Sponge: $750.00 – $900.00

A single-stemmed rose in full bloom, posing as if just gathered from grandmother's garden, graces each side. Very plain form accented only by raised blue-highlighted bands around the top and bottom characterizes the Old Fashioned Garden Rose pitcher. Diffused blue highlighting provides focus for the rose stem. Notice that the applied handle is attached quite high on this pitcher.

Peacock

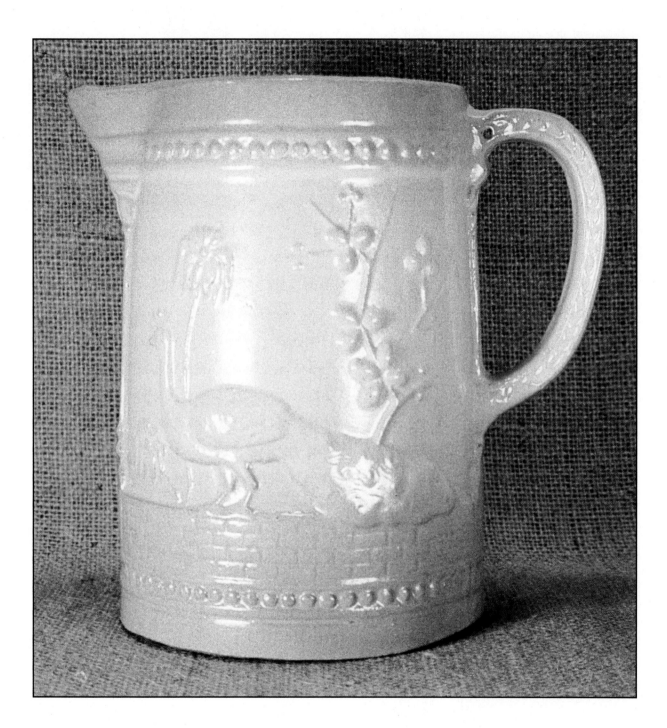

SIZE: 8½"h, 5"w (bottom)
AVAILABILITY: Extremely rare pattern
COLORS: Blue and white, Rockingham glaze, yellow ware
MINT VALUES: Blue and white: $600.00 – $800.00
Rockingham glaze: $200.00 – $250.00
Yellowware: $600.00 – $800.00

The graceful peacock with its long, flowing tail ambles on a brick path amidst a setting of urns, columns, and palm trees. Pearl beading surrounds the top and bottom of the pitcher and also provides accent for the applied handle. Good mold patterns and pale blue diffusing around the top and bottom are characteristic of the Peacock pitcher.

Columns are strategically placed on each side of the pitcher to creatively camouflage the mold seams.

The Peacock pattern is noted as one of the most elegant of this utilitarian ware. Consistent pale blue coloring is typical for most Peacock items which include a bowl, salt holder, and custard cup along with a pitcher shown in the grouping below. Butter holders and coffee pots were also produced in this pattern.

 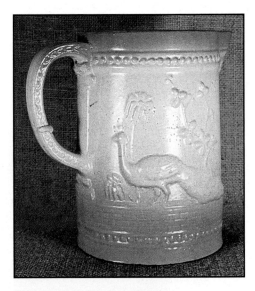

Pinecone

The simple design of the Pinecone pitcher makes it an attractive part of any collection. The smooth body is accented by a simple vertical branch with pinecones attached. Simple molded bands surround the base with a linking pattern surrounding the top. Blue diffusing highlights the pinecones on each side as well as the top and bottom rims. The applied handle is placed high on the pitcher's side.

SIZE: 9¼"h, 5¾"w (bottom)
AVAILABILITY: Extremely rare pattern
COLORS: Blue and white
MINT VALUE: $500.00 – $600.00

∽——Pirate——∽

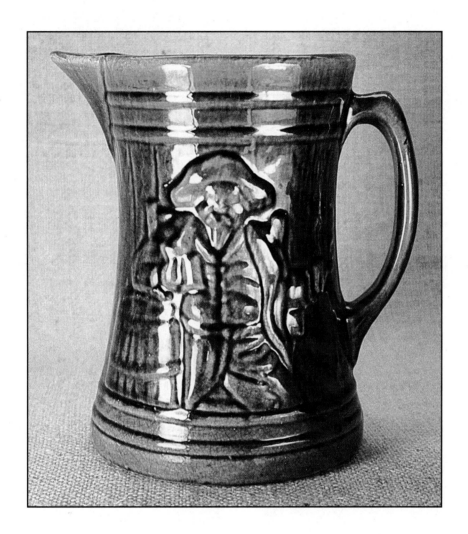

SIZE:	8"h, 6"w (bottom)
AVAILABILITY:	Common
COLORS:	Solid green
MINT VALUE:	$175.00 – $200.00

    Sitting against a background of vertical planks with his right arm resting on a staved barrel and tankard in hand, the pirate is apparently enjoying the solitude between action-packed adventures. With a tri-cornered hat, goatee, and garb appropriate for the occasion, only a patch over one eye is needed to fit the imagery one has of these sea-going marauders. The pirate is also enjoying a cigar in his right hand with the mold pattern showing even the curling smoke billowing upward. The slender mid-section of the pitcher flares downward and upward with simple mold bands accenting the top and bottom. While only seen in solid green, the Pirate pitcher may have been produced in other colors also. Although examples are not shown, matching mugs were also produced.

Plain Pitchers with Banding and Diffusing

SIZE: 9"h, 5"w (top left and right)
AVAILABILITY: Common; rare coloration, left
COLORS: Blue and white
MINT VALUES: $200.00 – $250.00 (right)
$275.00 – $300.00 (left)

SIZE: 8½"h, 6½"w (bottom left and right)
AVAILABILITY: Common
COLORS: Blue and white, blue and tan
MINT VALUE: $200.00 – $250.00

Pitchers with very plain form were often accented very simply with bands of blue either distinctly applied, as with the example at left above, or applied in a diffusing manner like the other examples shown. Tan clay (bottom right) is accented with bands of dark blue diffusing in the same pitcher form as the pristine white Bristol glazed example (bottom left) which has a different personality with the wider bands of medium blue diffusing. The more straight-sided example at top right generates a handsome appearance with the very high contrast between the white glazed clay and the dark blue diffused bands.

∽─── Plain Pitchers with Swirling and Transfers ───∽

SIZE: 8½"h, 5½"w (examples above)
AVAILABILITY: Common form, rare coloration
COLORS: Blue and white
MINT VALUE: $175.00 – $225.00 each

Two examples of pitchers with basically plain form accented with downward sweeping bands of blue diffusing are shown above. The blue swirls on the simple ovoid shape at left have a darker slate appearance on the tan clay. The example at right has very pale blue diffusing around the top and bottom as well as subtle wide swirls across the bulbous bottom.

Very plain pitcher forms are accented not only with distinctive bands of diffused blue around the rim and base but also with rose cluster transfers. The transfer pattern shown here is more commonly seen on washstand pieces rather than on these pitcher forms which would have been used in the kitchen or possibly as more decorative wares for serving.

SIZES: Large: 9"h, 5"w; Small: 6½"h, 5"w
AVAILABILITY: Rare, not commonly seen
COLORS: Blue and white
MINT VALUE: $275.00 – $325.00 each

Poinsettia

SIZE: 6"h, 6"w (at widest point)
AVAILABILITY: Common pattern
COLORS: Blue and white, brown
MINT VALUE: Blue and white: $225.00 – $275.00
Brown: $125.00 – 150.00

Two large poinsettias adorn each side of this pitcher which has a unique background pattern of caning around its very short, rounded body. The close pair of vertical and horizontal lines forming the cane background are accented with a small circle at each intersection. A simple braided band encircles the narrow collar while the applied handle gently curves upward and inward to reach the connection with the collar. The Poinsettia pattern notoriously has a fairly shallow mold pattern; yet, coloration is consistent as evidenced on the examples shown.

Rose on Trellis

SIZES: Large: 9"h, 6"w (at widest point)
Medium: 8"h, 5½"w (at widest point)
Small: 7"h, 5"w (at widest point)
AVAILABILITY: Common pattern
COLORS: Blue and white, blue and tan
MINT VALUE: $225.00 – $275.00 each

Featuring a scene straight out of an old fashioned garden, the Rose on Trellis pattern is embossed over the entire exterior of the bulbous bottomed pitcher. A climbing bush having several open roses provides the focal point on each side. Most commonly seen in the slate blue and tan color scheme, the pitcher was also produced in white with pale blue diffused bands around the top and bottom (facing page). While only three sizes are known, the pitcher may have been produced in a larger and a smaller size. The Rose on Trellis pattern was also used on washstand sets although no examples are shown in that section.

Scrolls

SIZE: 7"h, 5"w
AVAILABILITY: Scarce pattern
COLORS: Blue and white
MINT VALUE: $225.00 – $250.00

Almost characteristic of a simple Grecian urn, the shape of this pitcher is accented with a narrow collar band of scrolling with draped panels extending downward over the hipped body. The lip and rim flare outward from the narrow collar to provide further modest form. The applied handle has a slight thumb grip at the top. Pale blue coloration almost covers the entire body with only a slight hint of white around the middle.

Scrolls and Feathers

SIZE: 7"h, 6"w
AVAILABILITY: Extremely rare pattern
COLORS: Blue and white
MINT VALUE: $350.00 – $400.00

The Scrolls and Feathers pitcher captures elegant style for a type of pottery which was produced and intended for common, everyday usage. Its straight-sided form is stylishly accented by a gracefully arched and well-defined pouring spout.

Large sweeps of overstated scrolling with a feathered pattern extend downward from the rim and upward from the base around the entire body. Even the applied handle has a touch of class with scrolling at the lower attachment point. Excellent mold pattern is typical of the Scrolls and Feathers pattern which is very simply accented with bands of blue diffusing around the top and bottom.

Scroll and Leaf

The Scroll and Leaf pitcher has the same basic shape as the Scrolls and Feathers pitcher seen above. A similar yet distinctively different pattern characterizes this pitcher which may have been specifically designed to accommodate promotional messages, such as this one for Mallett's Grocery in Lexington, Nebraska. A repeating band of overstated scrolls highlighted in blue accents the top rim with elegantly embossed and highlighted leaf tips surrounding the bottom. The applied handle carries out the scrolling theme with its lower attachment.

SIZE: 7"h, 6"w
AVAILABILITY: Extremely rare pattern
COLORS: Blue and white
MINT VALUES: $300.00 – $350.00
$450.00 – $500.00 with advertising

∾—— Sea Captain ——∾

SIZES: Pitcher: 8½"h, 5½"w
Mugs: 5"h, 3½"w
AVAILABILITY: Scarce pattern
COLORS: Brown, blue
MINT VALUES: Pitcher: $175.00 – $225.00
Mugs: $40.00 – $45.00 each

Framed in a vine and leaves medallion, the profile of a stately Dutch sea captain with a crook-stemmed pipe in his mouth embellishes one side of this pitcher while the same medallion style frames a windmill on the other side. A vertical pattern of compass points accents each side of the medallions. The distinct mold even allows the sea captain's mustache to be seen. Air bubbles were often trapped when clay was pressed into the molds, causing pits to occur in the finished exterior. An example of such a pit can be seen on the sea captain's cheek. The actual color of the finished product was often a surprise with uniformity and consistency being unusual rather than the rule. The color difference between this Sea Captain pitcher and the matching mugs bears such an example which was true in all colors, even the more reliable cobalt oxide used for blue and white pieces. Notice that the zinc oxide used for the interior is carried slightly over the exterior rim on both the pitcher and mugs.

Shield

SIZE: 8"h, 5"w
AVAILABILITY: Scarce pattern
COLORS: Blue and white, brown
MINT VALUE: Blue and white: $250.00 – $300.00
Brown: $75.00 – 100.00

The pattern of the Shield pitcher almost has the appearance of an optical illusion and may have been a forerunner design to the Art Deco movement. The bulbous shield design narrows at top and bottom where connected to bands of mold rings. Half shields appear to overlap the predominant shield creating a vertical pattern of seemingly intertwined lines. Deep blue diffusing around the top and bottom provides framing for the shield embossing. The Shield pitcher was also produced with a brown glaze.

Sleepy Eye

SIZES: 10"h, 7"w
8"h, 6"w
7"h, 5"w
6"h, 4"w
4¾"h, 4¾"w
AVAILABILITY: Rare pattern
COLORS: Blue and white
MINT VALUES: $250.00 – $300.00 each

The Sleepy Eye Milling Company, Sleepy Eye, Minnesota, used this portrait in its advertising from 1883 to 1921. The pitchers were given away as premiums along with other items. They were made by the Western Stoneware Company and other potteries and were originally produced in five sizes along with a mug version. The famous dark blue Indian in headdress on a plain pure white background provides the focal point for the front side while tepees and trees are featured on the other side. From a larger base, the pitcher has a slight upward tapering and a gracefully overstated lip. The dark blue highlighted handle repeats the Indian head motif with a unique thumb grip. Although these pitchers have been heavily reproduced, they are easily detected since reproductions are quite lightweight with thin ceramic-like construction.

Spongeware Pitchers

SIZE: 9"h, 5"w
AVAILABILITY: Extremely rare pattern
COLORS: Blue and white
MINT VALUE: $550.00 – $600.00

A rarely seen chain-link sponging pattern was used to decorate the plain-sided pitcher above. The side view above right shows how the maker intended for the pattern to continue on the handle.

SIZE: 8"h, 8"w
AVAILABILITY: Extremely rare form
COLORS: Blue and white
MINT VALUE: $1,700.00 – $2,000.00

Referred to as a vessel for holding either batter or beer, it is understandable how this large pitcher at right could be used for both. Its capacity would allow ample quantity for filling tankards several times. If used for batter, mixing could be done easily because of its large mouth which has a small pinched lip. The dark blue sponging enhances its attractiveness.

SIZE: Generally 8½" to 9"h, 5"w
AVAILABILITY: Common
COLORS: Blue and white
MINT VALUES: $250.00 – $300.00 each

Numerous examples of pitchers using sponging as the predominant form of decoration were produced. While the shapes and forms were quite similar, the sponging made each one distinctively different since it was applied by hand using a sponge dipped in color-laced glaze. Unloading a kiln was especially a treat and a surprise for makers producing spongewares since the result of their artistry would not be known until firing was completed.

Although widely produced, each sponge-ware pitcher is uniquely different. Some makers preferred closer, more dense sponging while others preferred larger, more open sponging. Evenly repeating patterns, such as the example shown above right using a repeating "chickenwire" pattern, were a challenge for the sponge artist.

SIZE: Generally 8½" to 9"h, 5"w
AVAILABILITY: Common
COLORS: Blue and white
MINT VALUES: $250.00 – $300.00 each

SIZE: 9"h, 5½"w
AVAILABILITY: Scarce
COLORS: Blue and white
MINT VALUE: $250.00 – $300.00

Different in shape from those previously shown, these two pitchers using sponging decoration illustrate the creativity mold makers used in keeping a variety of forms and styles available for their customers.

The ovoid shape at left is uniquely different from other pitcher forms. The plain body with a small pulled lip is accented only by all-over sponging.

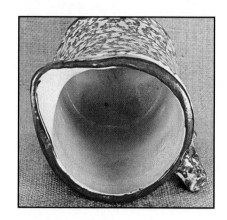

SIZE: 7"h, 5"w
AVAILABILITY: Common
COLORS: Blue and white, Rockingham glaze
MINT VALUES: $200.00 – $225.00, blue and white
$125.00 – $150.00, Rockingham glaze

The smaller pitcher shown above left has a unique handle design allowing for both a thumb grip and a pinky grip. The top view at right shows a band of blue around the top rim as additional decoration. Molded stoneware forms were produced not only in a variety of glaze colors but also in what is called Rockingham glaze as the example above left shows. Generally used on earlier wares, the brown and yellow colors of the Rockingham glaze were replaced because of preference for the blue and white as well as green and cream color combinations.

Stag and Pine Trees

SIZE: 8"h, 5½"w (bottom)
AVAILABILITY: Scarce
COLORS: Blue and tan
MINT VALUE: $250.00 – $300.00

The slate blue and tan coloration was consistently used on the Stag and Pine Trees pitcher. One side features a handsome stag majestically posing among forest undergrowth as if surveying his domain. The background illustrates the stag's native environment around the pitcher with a grouping of stately pine trees featured on the back side. The mottled background seems to characterize the roughness of the wild.

Swan

The intricately designed Swan pattern features a large center medallion of laurel sprigs, flowers, and ribbons on each side serving as a frame for the elegant swan floating gracefully. The mold pattern of the brown example above clearly shows the rippling water as well as several birds in flight over the swan. A diamond lattice background is enhanced by a band of harp-style scrolling around the top and onto the lip while the bottom is encircled by a repeating band of laurel sprigs. The applied handle is beaded.

SIZE: 8"h, 5½"w (bottom)
AVAILABILITY: Rare pattern
COLORS: Blue and white, brown, spongeware
MINT VALUES: Blue and white: $350.00 – $400.00
Spongeware: $1,000 – $1,500.00
Brown: $175.00 – $225.00

Several examples of the Swan pitcher in blue and white illustrate the color differences yielded sometimes by the typically more reliable cobalt oxide. Blue and white examples can range from quite pale, even lighter than the example at top left, to a quite rich, dark blue as shown by the example at bottom left. Interestingly, the Swan pitcher uses the same overall design as the Leaping Deer pitcher with the only difference being the pattern within the medallion.

Swastika

SIZE: 8½"h, 5½"w
AVAILABILITY: Common pattern
COLORS: Blue and white, brown
MINT VALUES: Blue and white: $200.00 – $250.00
Brown: $125.00 – $150.00

Although typically a faint pattern, a swastika is centered in a box border on an impressed dots background. The swastika is known as an Indian good luck sign. Bands of smaller reversed swastika symbols encircle the top rim and base. The heavy, rough background provides the only accenting other than bands of characteristically pale, diffused blue around the top and bottom. The applied handle has a pointed thumb grip at top. Brown examples are typically the same color all over.

Tulip

SIZE: 8"h, 4½"w
AVAILABILITY: Rare pattern
COLORS: Blue and white, multicolored
MINT VALUE: Blue and white, $300.00 – $350.00
Multicolored: $175.00 – $225.00

A dramatically flowing tulip in full bloom provides the focal point for this pitcher. Accented with a wide band of scrolling around the top and a mold band around the bottom, the tulip is highlighted in blue. The top and base are also highlighted with bands of diffused blue. The applied handle has an interesting scrolled thumb grip on top. The dark spot just above the top handle attachment on the example top right is a mass of dark glaze on the pitcher's surface which was probably one of the surprises often discovered when pieces were removed from the kiln.

The example at bottom right is often referred to as Early Roseville. The green and orange coloration is particularly striking on this pattern.

Wildflower

SIZE: 9"h, 5"w
AVAILABILITY: Rare pattern
COLORS: Blue and white
MINT VALUE: $200.00 – $250.00

A very plain white background is simply accented with narrow bands of blue and a stenciled wildflower design. The stenciled design appears at top and bottom on both sides with the design repeated at the bottom below the applied handle and the spout. The top rim is also accented with a narrow band of blue.

Wild Rose

A stem of fully opened wild roses graces a smooth white background on each side of this pitcher. With the wild roses highlighted in deep blue and sponging around the top and bottom as well as on the handle, this example is unique. This combination of highlighted pattern accented with sponging is not seen on other pitchers.

SIZE: 9"h, 6½"w
AVAILABILITY: Extremely rare pattern, more commonly seen in spongeware
COLORS: Blue and white, rarely seen in green and cream
MINT VALUE: $450.00 – $500.00 (all colors)

While the sponged example is an outstanding part of any collection, the intricate pattern detailing of the Wild Rose pitcher is most clearly seen on the piece at left. The embossing is so distinct on this example that the veins in the leaves can be seen. Double rows of beading separate the flower stem from the collar and base patterns above and below it. The beading is repeated on the sides of the applied handle. A mirror-image pattern of semi-circles with diamonds between accents the base while a band of smaller wild roses and leaves accents the collar.

The Wild Rose pitcher is very rarely seen in a green and cream color combination with the flower stem highlighted in green with diffused green around the top and bottom.

Another example of the sponged Wild Rose pattern shows slightly less dense sponging around the top and base while the handle on the same example at right is very closely sponged.

Windy City

Known under the names Windy City and Fannie Flagg, this pitcher particularly commemorated the windy city of Chicago in the early 1900s. Produced by the Robinson Clay Pottery Company of Akron, Ohio, it may have specifically commemorated the reconstruction of Chicago after the great fire started by Mrs. O'Leary and her cow, as the story goes.

Numerous molded stoneware pieces and patterns were produced in this blue and gray coloration which is a subject unto itself and different from the pottery produced in blue and white. This popular Windy City pitcher is shown as an example of this color and style. Collectors can certainly specialize in just these types of items, many of which feature intricate outdoor themes.

"Fannie" (the lady on the front side) is dressed in her finest turn-of-the-century attire and apparently was proud to stroll the streets of the reborn city even though the gusting wind is whipping up her frock.

The opposite side of the pitcher features a Chicago skyscraper which appears to be triangular in shape. Block columns accent each side of the pitcher with the side seam and spout camouflaged with a vertical scalloping pattern.

SIZE:	9"h, 5"w
AVAILABILITY:	Scarce pattern
COLORS:	Blue and gray
MINT VALUE:	$450.00 – $500.00

Small fluted scallops further accent the pouring spout. The separately molded and applied handle simulates a tree branch which provides for interesting symbolism. Matching mugs were also produced in the Windy City pattern.

Section II – Coffee and Tea Pots

In today's age of instant beverages and automatic drip coffee makers, it is hard to imagine perking coffee or brewing tea in one of these now-prized swirl pots. This section focuses on the limited line of coffee and tea pots which were produced in the blue and white molded stoneware. While tea pots have been widely produced in media from stoneware to fine china, stoneware coffee pots are much less prevalent. Blue and white was apparently the color combination of choice for coffee and tea pots since the styles of vessels included in this section are not usually found in other colors.

Coffee pots typically had a metal cap on the bottom which aided in the transfer of heat and protected the clay portion of the pot. Loose tea leaves or loose coffee grounds were "brewed" on the wood-burning cookstove and strained when served. For the more practical user of one's "fine pottery," coffee may have been made in a metal pot and transferred to the swirl pot for serving. With the help of the metal base cap, the pot could be left on the stove to keep its contents warm.

It is amazing that any still survive, particularly with the exposure to the heat and high usage which they received as utilitarian wares. Even a missing metal plate does not diminish much value from a piece.

Coffee and tea pots rarely surface in the market place today; their simple scarcity causes prices to be rather high. A coffee pot and a tea pot in a collection are true prizes and are typically some of the most valuable pieces for any collection. Today, pots such as these grace shelves, not stovetops, in tribute to a different era.

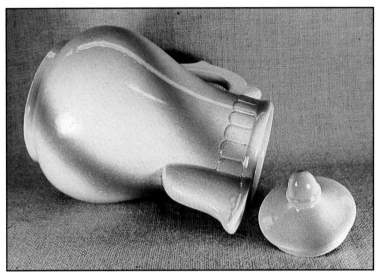

ᳬᜒ————Peacock Coffee Pot————ᜒᳬ

Of all shapes and forms of molded stoneware, the Peacock coffee pot is perhaps the most rare. Consistency in coloration and form make the Peacock pattern one of the most elegant of these utilitarian wares. Holding true to the light blue and white coloring, this Peacock coffee pot has exceedingly clear mold marks which are so crisp that one can almost imagine the graceful peacock strolling along the brick pathway under the stately palm trees.

SIZE: 10"h (with lid),
6¼"w (at base),
7"w (handle to spout)
AVAILABILITY: Extremely rare pattern
COLORS: Blue and white only
MINT VALUE: $2,500.00 – $3,000.00

As one of the rarest, most desirable, most graceful, and most valuable pieces in any collection, the Peacock coffee pot was designed to be quite utilitarian with an extended lid base to prevent it from tipping off during pouring and to serve as a strainer in the spout. The top and bottom as well as the handle are defined with rows of beading, and the peacock pattern graces both sides of the pot. This example is from the collection of Ted and Sandra Gleason.

Oval Coffee Pot

SIZE: 10½"h (with lid), 4½"w, handle, 9"l
AVAILABILITY: Extremely rare pattern
COLORS: Blue and white only
MINT VALUE: $1,200.00 – $1,500.00

The Oval coffee pot is characterized by straight sides and a large oval diffused blue medallion in the center of each side. A coffee pot in this pattern is extremely rare, and even examples in less than mint condition can command quite high prices. The example shown has some discoloration possibly due to having had a prolonged close encounter with red dirt. As well, the metal base cap of this example is missing.

Swirl Coffee Pot

SIZE: 10"h (with lid), 6"w (at widest part near bottom)
AVAILABILITY: Rare pattern
COLORS: Blue and white only
MINT VALUE: $800.00 – $1,200.00

A Swirl coffee pot is a quite desirable piece for any collection. With a gracefully spurred handle, curved pouring spout, and an acorn finial, this example is, by definition, in near mint condition. Since it is missing the metal base cap, its value would be reduced from that which could be expected for a complete piece.

In mint condition complete with metal base cap, this Swirl coffee pot has excellent coloration. Light to dark variations in the blue swirls can be expected among different examples found. The deep rimmed lip for the lid with ball finial can be observed in the photo above right.

With its original metal base cap, the graceful blue swirls are accented at the top with a raised band of reverse rounded pickets. Both acorn and round ball styles of finials were used on the lids for Swirl coffee pots.

Swirl Coffee Pot (Large Size)

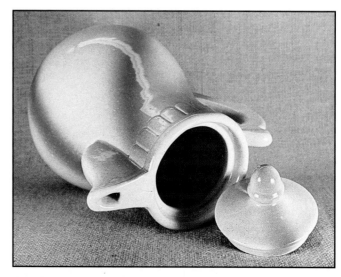

SIZE: 12"h (with lid), 8"w
(at widest part near bottom);
6"w (bottom)
AVAILABILITY: Rare pattern
COLORS: Blue and white only
MINT VALUE: $1,500.00 – $1,700.00

Because of its large size, this Swirl coffee pot may have been a restaurant version. There has been some discussion that this could even be a reproduction. Having examined the piece, it is the positon of the authors that it may simply be a later piece. While sharing the same styling with the smaller size, some differences are apparent, particularly the absence of a metal base cap and a flat, less graceful handle. Blue color variations are quite wide as is evident in the photo at right which also provides a comparison of the large-sized Swirl with the regular-sized coffee pot.

❧———— Swirl Tea Pot ————❧

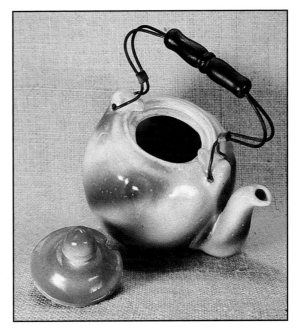

SIZE: 8½"h (with lid), 8"w (at widest part)
AVAILABILITY: Extremely rare pattern
COLORS: Blue and white only
MINT VALUE: $1,200.00 – $1,500.00

Rich dark blue and distinctive swirls accent this tea pot with a gooseneck spout. A unique double-wire is attached to pulled clay ears on each side of the top opening. The notched acorn finial lid is held in place by a small wing extending inward from the rim.

A Swirl tea pot is a most desirable addition for any collection. The example above left with acorn finial has lighter and more narrow swirls as compared with the pot bottom left with darker, more diffused swirls and a round knob finial. This example also has a small chip on the right handle attachment which would reduce its condition from mint and thus affect its value. A band of raised bubbles encircles the top of the tea pot which does not have a metal base cap as the coffee pot does.

∽——Spongeware Tea Pot——∽

SIZE:	8½"h (with lid), 8½" (at widest part near bottom)
AVAILABILITY:	Extremely rare pattern
COLORS:	Blue and white only
MINT VALUE:	$1,200.00 − $1,500.00

While spongeware pitchers are fairly common, spongeware tea pots certainly are not. This unique example is sponged all over in dark blue. The deep lid fits securely so as not to tip over when pouring.

∽——Blue Banded Coffee Pot——∽

SIZE:	9"h (with lid), 8" (at widest part near bottom)
AVAILABILITY:	Scarce
COLORS:	Blue and white only
MINT VALUE:	$650.00 − $750.00

This unusual coffee pot is low and compact. Its simple, graceful, and functional form is characterized by its coloration with bands of blue and white with a blue lid. Groups of incised lines accent the base.

Section III – Mugs

Today we reach for glasses to serve cool lemonade on a Sunday afternoon and ceramic mugs for a cup of hot chocolate on a snowy winter evening. Prior to the inexpensive mass production of drinking glasses and everyday mugs, stoneware mugs were the vessel of choice for almost any beverage.

Mugs were produced in a variety of styles and patterns with many complementing the pitchers so that one could amass the number of beverage holders thought needed to serve guests when entertaining on a Sunday afternoon or other special occasions or even for everyday use. Sets including the pitcher and matching mugs are quite desirable today and often difficult for collectors to gather, particularly in matching colors. Remember,

molded stoneware was basically inexpensive and was typically used on an everyday basis. Fine china and porcelain was generally used for "dress up" occasions.

Merchants, pubs, and inns found molded stoneware to be an inexpensive promotional item as well as an inexpensive and durable container for serving hot and cool beverages. Mugs identifying establishments or having advertising messages are quite unique pieces.

Mugs add variety and spice to any aficionado's collection; in fact, mugs can certainly be a focus for some collectors while others may even specialize only in those with promotional messages.

A color-matched set of Flying Birds mugs is a rare part of any collection. It often takes years to accumulate such a collection as these six shown above.

⤳——Advertising Mugs——⤨

SIZE: 4¾"h, 3¼"w
AVAILABILITY: Scarce
COLORS: Blue and white
MINT VALUE: $100.00 – $125.00 each

Although simplistic in style, an advertising logo adds value to any piece. "Allison's Wells" could be advertising a business or a popular tavern.

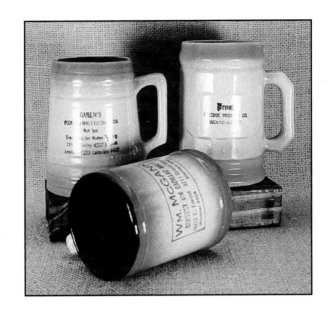

Advertising mugs are seen in a variety of styles and with a variety of messages; these are simply examples of the many available. The "Wm. McGann" mug is interesting with its brown glazed interior.

	Garens (left)	McGann (center)	Frost (right)
SIZES:	5"h, 4"w	4½"h, 3"w	5½"h, 3"w
AVAILABILITY:	Scarce	Scarce	Scarce
COLORS:	Blue/white	Blue/white/brown	Blue/white
MINT VALUE:	$150.00 – $175.00	$150.00 – $175.00	$150.00 – $175.00

SIZE:	4¾"h, 4"w
AVAILABILITY:	Scarce
COLORS:	Blue and white
MINT VALUE:	$100.00 – $125.00

This mug advertises Riker's (101 Main St., Hackensack, NJ) and was probably used for serving favorite beverages in that establishment. The barrel style is highlighted in diffused blue around the top. An applied handle is on the opposite side from the message.

This handsome duo of an advertising pitcher on the right and smaller malt syrup mug on the left typifies the variety of molded stoneware used for promotional purposes.

	Malt syrup pitcher (left)	G. A. Gohlmann pitcher (right)
SIZE:	5"h, 3½"w	6"h, 4½"w
AVAILABILITY:	Scarce	Scarce
COLORS:	Blue/white	Blue/white/brown
MINT VALUE:	$150.00 – $175.00	$150.00 – $175.00

Green Barrel Mugs

SIZE: 5"h, 3¼"w
AVAILABILITY: Common
COLORS: Solid green
MINT VALUE: $35.00 – $50.00 each

This barrel-shaped mug features raised bands circling the bulbous body. Rich green color adds to its attractiveness.

Mugs Grouping

A collection of mug patterns and styles are shown at right. From left: Banded Mug, Flying Birds Mug, Cherry Cluster Mug, Plain Diffused Blue Mug. The middle two are presented again later.

Banded mug (left)		Plain diffused blue mug (right)	
SIZE:	5"h, 3½"w	SIZE:	5"h, 3½"w
AVAILABILITY:	Common	AVAILABILITY:	Common
COLORS:	Blue and white	COLORS:	Blue and tan
MINT VALUE:	$95.00 – $125.00 each	MINT VALUE:	$95.00 – $125.00 each

Basketweave and Morning Glory Mugs

SIZE: 5"h, 3"w
AVAILABILITY: Scarce
COLORS: Blue and white, solid green
MINT VALUES: Blue and white: $150.00 – $175.00 each
Solid green: $50.00 – $75.00 each

The basketweave pattern is accented by an upwardly sweeping stem of morning glories and leaves. The squared handle allows for easy gripping.

Three variations of Basketweave and Morning Glory mugs are shown at right. From left, blue and white, solid green, and blue and white with flowers and leaves outlined in gold.

Cherry Cluster Mug

SIZE: 5"h, 3"w
AVAILABILITY: Extremely rare
COLORS: Blue and white
MINT VALUE: $275.00 – $325.00 each

The Cherry Cluster mug has the same pattern as the pitcher by that name. The cherry cluster appears on both sides on a waffle background. The spurred and beaded handle is also unusual for a mug. A band of leaves encircles the top and bottom. A set of these and a pitcher of the same pattern would be almost priceless!

Dutch Boy and Girl Mug

One side of this mug features a stenciled Dutch boy (right) while the other side has a stenciled Dutch girl (left). Dark blue bands encircle the top and bottom of the mug.

SIZE: 4"h, 3¼"w
AVAILABILITY: Rare pattern
COLORS: Blue and white
MINT VALUE: $150.00 – $175.00 each

The Dutch Boy and Girl pattern was used on a variety of wares including a pitcher and an extremely rare rolling pin.

Flying Birds Mugs

SIZE: 4½"h, 3"w
AVAILABILITY: Scarce
COLORS: Blue and white
MINT VALUE: $175.00 – $200.00 each

The pattern on the Flying Birds mug is identical on both sides with slight tapering from top to bottom. The top and bottom are banded with rows of small flowers. Mugs are generally found in medium blue with diffusing variations.

A grouping of mugs with the matching pitcher is shown above left. The Lovebirds pattern embellishes one side of the pitcher as shown while the Flying Birds motif is used on the other side.

This matched set of Flying Birds mugs has probably taken years to acquire by purchasing one at a time and trading along the way to match colors.

Grape Cluster in Shield Mugs

A cluster of grapes in a shield appears on each side of this mug. A band of ribbing around the top and bottom accented by rows of arrows and beading provides a frame for an almost bark-like background. Examples are shown on the following page in several color variations, including green and cream, yellow, dark green, and teal. This pattern is rarely seen in blue and white.

SIZE: 5"h, 3"w
AVAILABILITY: Common
COLORS: Green and cream, solid green, yellow
MINT VALUE: $50.00 – $75.00 each

Grape Cluster in Shield Pitcher and Mug Sets

A challenge for any collector is to assemble a set of mugs to accompany a matching pitcher. The challenge is even greater to assemble a color-matched set, particularly in green, since so much variation occurred with the copper oxide used to achieve that color. Even with slight color variations, a complete Grape Cluster in Shield set, whether in the green and cream combination or in solid green, is a stunning set. The value for a complete set such as these shown would be approximately 25 percent higher than for individual pieces purchased separately.

Sleepy Eye Mug

SIZE: 5"h, 3"w
AVAILABILITY: Rare
COLORS: Blue and white
MINT VALUE: $275.00 – $300.00 each

The Sleepy Eye mug at right provides a portrait of the famous dark blue Indian in headdress on a pure white background. The Indian is nestled among trees and bushes at the base. Notice that the handle is highlighted in dark blue and has a gripping knob at its top.

Sleepy Eye Stein

SIZE: 8"h, 4"w
AVAILABILITY: Extremely rare
COLORS: Blue and gray
MINT VALUE: $800.00 – $1,000.00

A variation of the Sleepy Eye pattern is presented below in the form of a stein with blue and gray coloring. One side of the stein features a stoic Indian, and the other side depicts tepees in a field. Notice the Indian head used as a spur on the handle as well as the fine detailing around the base of the stein.

Various Mugs and Tumblers

Spongeware Mug and Tumbler

The small mug at left with footed base is seen in a rich dark blue sponge. Notice that the sponge detailing is carried inside the rim of the cup as well as on the outside of the handle.

The simple, plain tumbler at right has a band of diffused blue around the bottom and is accented with gold around the lip.

	Mug		Tumbler
SIZE:	4½"h, 4"w	SIZE:	4½"h, 3½"w
AVAILABILITY:	Scarce	AVAILABILITY:	Scarce
COLORS:	Blue and white	COLORS:	Blue and white
MINT VALUE:	$175.00 – $200.00 each	MINT VALUE:	$75.00 – $100.00 each

Stenciled Wildflower Mug

The stenciled wildflower pattern appears on both sides of this mug which has a plain white background. A dark blue band decorates the top rim and base of the mug. The handle features a generously flared grip.

SIZE:	4½"h, 4"w
AVAILABILITY:	Scarce
COLORS:	Blue and white
MINT VALUE:	$150.00 – $175.00 each

Sponge and Faces Mugs

The sponge example above at left has a pattern that is not distinguishable.

The solid blue mug at right features a woman's face on one side and a man's face on the other side. Spurred handles enhance each mug.

SIZE:	5"h, 3½"w
AVAILABILITY:	Rare (for Faces)
COLORS:	Blue and white
MINT VALUE:	$175.00 – $200.00, Sponge
	$100.00 – $125.00, Faces

Section IV – Butter and Pastry Crocks

Butter holders were designed to hold a very common household staple — freshly churned butter. The contents of these holders seems like a simple enough item, but let's reflect on an earlier time when having butter on the table did not mean simply opening the refrigerator. In fact, imagine the storage of anything that needed to be kept cool. Butter, milk, and other perishables would spoil quickly in the old days if not kept cool. Storage might mean keeping perishables in a nearby creek, spring, or stream or in a "milk well," a hole dug in the ground for cool storage.

Later came the ice box. Large chunks of ice were bought quite frequently during warm weather and placed in the ice box to keep items cool. A drip pan in the bottom of the box had to be emptied as the ice melted. Those living in towns used an ice delivery service, whereas those living in the country added ice gathering as a regular chore during the winter. Blocks of ice were cut from nearby ponds, rivers or streams. Once cut, they would be wrapped in burlap and packed in hay or straw deep in the ground, where they could be stored quite a while. Having ice and cool storage space took a lot of work. When looking at the beauty of restored ice boxes today, remember the tasks associated with their use.

It is also appropriate to stop and reflect on the era during which these utilitarian wares were used. Producing one's own butter typically meant that a household had their own cow. Those who did not own a "Bossy" purchased dairy products from local producers.

Cows were milked twice daily, in the early morning and in the late afternoon when the cows returned from pasture. To produce well, the cows had to eat well. While we may savor french onion dips today, cows were notorious for producing their own version when grazing in a field of wild onions; "french onion milk" was certainly not considered a delicacy in earlier days.

Thus, pastures were well-tended to provide good products for the family and for sale. Once gathered, raw milk would be strained to remove obvious impurities; those less than obvious ones are now handled through pasteurization.

Milk was the source for many by-products, including butter, cheese, and whipped cream. For butter making, milk was allowed to clabber (curdle or sour) in milk crocks with the process hastened by placing them in a warm spot. Once clabbered, the milk was placed in a churn, most of which are quite collectible today.

The churning action coagulated the butter which could be gathered in lumps from the liquid. The butter was then "worked" or kneaded to remove excess liquid, lightly salted, and molded or placed in crocks for use in the kitchen. Butter molds and prints are other items highly collected today. This laborious process was often a chore repeated several times weekly in order to keep this staple product available for cooking or flavoring a batch of hot, homemade biscuits. And what happened to the excess liquid from the churning process? Another staple for the table — buttermilk!

Butter holders held quantities for kitchen use and many were placed on the serving table. Glass butter dishes often held molded cakes of butter or those decorated with butter prints. For those purchasing butter from their favorite farm, butter containers were returned and refilled, as were milk bottles.

People living during this era were hard workers, and women typically spent most of their time preparing meals and looking after the household. While butter seems like such a simple commodity today, it was a necessary ingredient for practically every meal and required hard work to get it to the table. A prized product and its simple, utilitarian container give us greater appreciation for the variety of patterns of butter holders seen today.

Apple Blossom Butter Holder

SIZE: 5"h, 6½"w
AVAILABILITY: Extremely rare
COLORS: Blue and white
MINT VALUE: $750.00 – $800.00

The Apple Blossom butter holder has a large cluster of flowers and leaves that virtually covers all sides of the crock. Both sides are identical. Rows of beads surround the top and bottom of the crock as well as the outside edge of the lipped lid. A band of leaves surrounds the recessed knob on the lid which fits snugly over a raised rim on the crock.

Apple Blossom Pastry Crock

SIZE: 6"h, 8"w
AVAILABILITY: Extremely rare
COLORS: Blue and white
MINT VALUE: $900.00 – $1,000.00

The Apple Blossom pastry crock is larger than the butter holder. A large highlighted starburst adorns each side seam where the handles are attached. Rows of beads surround the top and bottom of the crock as well as the outside edge of the lipped lid. Butter holders and pastry crocks were frequently produced in the same pattern and often marketed by their producers as two-, three-, and five-pound butter containers. The larger size is denoted in this section as pastry crocks which were used for food storage and holding butter and quantities of pie crust. As needed for daily baking, dough could be taken from the crock and rolled for baking pies using whatever fruit was in season.

∽——Apricot with Honeycomb Butter Holder——∽

SIZE: 4"h, 7"w
AVAILABILITY: Common pattern
COLORS: Blue and white, green and cream
MINT VALUE: $200.00 – $250.00

The Apricot with Honeycomb pattern graced butter crocks as well as pitchers, salt holders, bowls, and milk crocks. Found in blue and white as well as in green and cream, colors range from more pale shades to dark, rich hues. The apricot cluster on either side of "BUTTER" usually provides the base for color highlighting as is seen on these examples.

"BUTTER" is highlighted on some examples while it is the background color on others. An interesting characteristic of most butter crocks using the lid over a raised rim style is that while the inside of the crock base is glazed, the inside of the lid is not. Consequently, the inside of most butter crocks, having received any usage, will smell quite rancid. Replacement bails are shown on each of these examples.

Variations in colors and highlighting are quite typical among examples as shown here. The mold patterns of these examples are quite distinct. The lid has a pattern of wide pickets around the side edge with honeycomb providing a background on the top for a circle of scrolling. The recessed knob is very thin and hard to grasp, possibly explaining why many lids were broken.

Basketweave and Daisy Butter Holder

SIZE:	4½"h, 6½"w
AVAILABILITY:	Extremely rare pattern
COLORS:	Blue and white
MINT VALUE:	$350.00 – $400.00

On a basketweave background large daisies flank each side of dark blue "BUTTER" on the front with two daisies with crossed stems adorning the back. The basketweave pattern is highlighted in diffused blue around the top and bottom. Notice the very thick walls of the crock around its top rim. The bail is a replacement, and the piece may not have had a lid.

Basketweave and Morning Glory Butter Holder

SIZE: 4"h, 7¼"w
AVAILABILITY: Extremely rare pattern, not commonly seen
COLORS: Blue and white
MINT VALUE: $350.00 – $400.00

Deep mold markings are characteristic of the Basketweave and Morning Glory pattern. The word "BUTTER" is highlighted in dark blue on one side with the reverse side displaying a morning glory flower stem winding through the weave.

Note the slight color variations among the examples shown. Notice that the inside of this lid is glazed whereas most butter holder lid interiors were not; a narrow rim around the top exterior of the lid is not glazed.

The Basketweave and Morning Glory pattern was popularly used on a variety of wares. In groupings such as with the pitcher at right, this pattern is bold and striking.

Butterfly Pastry Crock and Butter Holder

Butterfly Pastry Crock
SIZE: 5"h, 8"w
AVAILABILITY: Scarce pattern
COLORS: Blue and white
MINT VALUE: $350.00 – $400.00

Butterfly Butter Holder
SIZE: 4¾"h, 5¾"w
AVAILABILITY: Scarce pattern
COLORS: Blue and white
MINT VALUE: $225.00 – $275.00

A large butterfly appears on the roughly textured orange peel background of these Butterfly crocks. Variations in pattern clarity occurred as the molds were worn because of frequent use. Four butterflies surround the sides of both the pastry crock shown at left and the butter holder shown at right. The butter holder lid is missing from the example shown which would affect its value as would the replaced wire bail. The wire bail inserts in holes on either side, not piercing the interior of the crock.

Chrysanthemum and Waffle Butter Holder

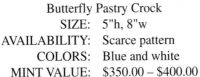

SIZE: Small, 4"h (with lid), 6"w
Large, 5"h, 6½"w
AVAILABILITY: Common
COLORS: Blue and white, green and cream, solid green
MINT VALUE: $125.00 – $175.00

A large chrysanthemum flower rests on a waffle background and appears four times around the perimeter of the crock. A band of small starbursts accents the top edge while the lid has two concentric bands of waffling.

This larger version of the Chrysanthemum and Waffle butter holder uses the green and cream color combination. The flower and starbursts bands are highlighted in green with the waffle background a natural cream color. This pattern was probably also produced in blue and white and solid blue. The lid is missing on the larger version, and neither size has a bail.

∾——**Cows and Fence Butter Holder**——∾

As would be typical in the pasture, the cows follow one another in a line around the body of the Cows and Fence butter crock. Starburst cornflowers with radiating bands of leaves frame the cows. "BUTTER" on this example is highlighted. The leaf and cornflower banding is repeated on the lid which fits snugly over an unglazed raised ring.

The original bail on this Cows and Fence butter crock fits into side holes which are a part of the mold. A rectangular basketweave grid found on the back of the crock represents a fence with the starburst cornflower and leaf banding at top and bottom.

SIZE:	4½"h (with lid), 7"w
AVAILABILITY:	Rare pattern
COLORS:	Blue and white only
MINT VALUE:	$450.00 – $500.00

Makers apparently had freedom of expression when it came to applying color since wide variations exist among examples. The cornflower and leaves pattern is repeated around the lid as seen above right.

While the cows received blue diffusing, "BUTTER" and the cornflowers were not highlighted by the maker of this example. Vertical ribbing surrounds the sides of the lid. The lid has a rather shallow knob which could account for a high amount of breakage.

⌁——Daisy Cluster Butter Holder——⌁

Four clusters of daisies surround the base of this crock while four small cosmos flowers decorate the top at intervals. The flowers on this example are highlighted in deep blue and stand out on the intricately detailed diamond background around the exterior. The bail attaches in side holes which do not pierce the interior. This example probably had a lid. A crack visible on the interior on the next page, top right, is an example of a factor which would reduce the piece's condition from mint to good and thus affect its value.

SIZE: 4½"h, 6"w
AVAILABILITY: Rare pattern
COLORS: Blue and white
MINT VALUE: $125.00 – $175.00

∽———Daisy and Waffle Butter Holder———∽

Color highlighting on the open daisy is typical on this pattern whether in blue and white or in green and cream. Coloring can range from light to dark in blue and green versions. Notice the light to dark green color variations on these examples. This variation was typical of the undependable nature of the copper oxide used to obtain green coloring.

SIZE: 4"h, 6"w
AVAILABILITY: Common
COLORS: Blue and white, solid blue,
       green and cream
MINT VALUE: $125.00 – $175.00

Four daisies on the trellis background surround the sides of the crock. Each daisy on this example with deep mold markings is generously highlighted with excellent blue coloring. The lid, with a slightly protruding rim inside, fits on top of the straight-sided crock. The lid, which is glazed on both sides, has a very shallow knob which is typical of most butter and pastry crocks. A narrow swirled band accents the top rim of the crock. The lid bears repeating bands of the trellis design.

Daisy and Trellis Butter Holder

SIZE:	4"h, 6"w
AVAILABILITY:	Common
COLORS:	Blue and white
MINT VALUE:	$125.00 – $175.00

The Daisy and Trellis butter holder pattern and form show only slight differences from the Daisy and Waffle design. Six large daisies on a close trellis background surround this crock which is almost solid blue. The trellis background is repeated on the lipped lid which fits snugly over a raised rim. The lid has a shallow recessed knob and is not glazed on the interior side. The replaced bail on this example fits into holes on either side which do not pierce the interior. The Daisy and Trellis pattern is quite similar to the Chrysanthemum and Trellis, the only difference being the type of flower and the decoration around the top rim.

Dragonfly and Flower Crocks

SIZE SHOWN: 4"h, 6"w
AVAILABILITY: Rare pattern
COLORS: Pale blue
MINT VALUE: $250.00 – $300.00 each

A dragonfly hovers on each side of an interesting flower design framed by a medallion of leaves. A diamond pattern border surrounds the top and base of the crock. A rounded and pointed picket design surrounds the top of the lid which has a recessed button knob. The same design is repeated on the lid's side which fits securely over a raised rim on the crock. Pale blue coloring is used consistently on this pattern.

According to an article by James L. Murphy entitled "Discovery of Photos Sheds New Light on Logan Pottery" (*AntiqueWeek*, July 17, 1995, page 15), the Dragonfly and Flower crocks were produced by the Logan Pottery Company in Logan, Ohio, "in 1, 2, 3, 4, 6, and 8 quart sizes, ranging in price from $1.32 to $4.00 a dozen ($1.98 to $6.00 crated)." Today a complete set would be nearly priceless — if found it could carry a tag of over $3,000. The one-quart size is included in the Utilitarian Kitchenwares Section as a grease jar. Based on the lingering smell, it was indeed used for that purpose.

Draped Windows Butter Holders and Pastry Crocks

	BUTTER HOLDER
SIZE:	4½"h, 8"w
AVAILABILITY:	Scarce
COLORS:	Blue and white,
	Blue and tan
MINT VALUE:	$175.00 – $225.00

	PASTRY CROCK
SIZE:	5"h, 6"w
AVAILABILITY:	Scarce
COLORS:	Blue and white,
	Blue and tan
MINT VALUE:	$225.00 – $275.00

Four windows draped with swags and embellished with scrolls at the bottom surround the crock. A dotted background pattern is encased by each window frame. The thin, flat lid for the pastry crock above has spoke-like markings. The lid above may be a replacement since it is different from those typically seen on the Draped Windows crocks. A marriage such as this would, of course, reduce its value.

The slate blue and tan color combination is used on the pair below which contrasts the sizes of the pastry crock (left) and the butter holder (right). Notice that the butter holder is slightly taller than the pastry crock.

Draped Windows Butter Holder

This butter holder with the blue and white color combination has an original lid with the inner and outer white and blue pattern rings repeating the texture inside the draped windows. A narrow unglazed ring separates the blue and white bands on the lid. The flat button knob is embellished with a flower design.

SIZE: 3¾"h, 5¾"w
AVAILABILITY: Scarce
COLORS: Solid green, possibly in blue and white, blue and tan
MINT VALUE: $125.00 – $150.00

Although the lid is missing, the dark green color and intense pattern make this smaller-sized butter holder with replaced bail an interesting piece.

Grape Cluster Pastry Crock

SIZE: 4¾"h (with lid), 8"w
AVAILABILITY: Rare
COLORS: Blue and white
MINT VALUE: $225.00 – $250.00 (with original lid)

A center cluster of grapes with leaves on each side appears on a diagonal trellis on this pastry crock with flanged handles. The lid on this example is a replacement since its original would have been slightly domed and would feature grape clusters on the diagonal trellis background. This pastry crock was most predominantly produced in what is called Early Roseville with vibrant green and orange coloring. A very small example in this pattern is included in the Bowls and Crocks section.

Eagle Butter Holder

SIZE: 6"h, 6"w
AVAILABILITY: Extremely rare
COLORS: Blue and white
MINT VALUE: $750.00 – $825.00

Impressed dots accented with roping and scrolling around the top and bottom serve as a classic background for the majestic eagle in flight clutching a shield and arrows. The scrolling is repeated around the top perimeter and side edge of the lipped lid which rests securely on a raised rim on the crock base. The bail on this example, which fits into side holes on the crock, has been replaced. The examples shown at right reflect slightly different coloration.

Fall Harvest Butter Holder and Pastry Crock

This unique pattern depicts its title by telling the purpose of the harvest in scenes encircling the crock. The idyllic story moves from a barn scene (bottom left) to grazing cows among trees (center) to hay stacks (bottom right). Notice the rail fence at the bottom edge and the scrolled columns at the side seams. Scrolling accents the top of the crock and is delicately repeated on the lid. The original bail is missing on the butter holder while the pastry crock never included a bail since the side holes were not punched.

Butter Holder (top left and bottom row)
SIZE: 4"h, 6"w
AVAILABILITY: Extremely rare
COLORS: Blue and white
MINT VALUE: $500.00 – $600.00

Pastry Crock (top right)
SIZE: 5½"h, 8"w
AVAILABILITY: Extremely rare
COLORS: Blue and white
MINT VALUE: $600.00 – $700.00

Indian and Tepee Butter Holder

This unique and extremely rare butter holder exudes detail and complex patterning. On one side two Indians in full headdress appear fresh from a successful deer hunt. The opposite side pictures a large tepee in grass with two Indians conversing on the left and a campfire on the right.

SIZE: 5"h, 6½"w
AVAILABILITY: Extremely rare
COLORS: Blue and white
MINT VALUE: $1,200.00 – $1,500.00

Smaller tepees can be seen in the background. A large branching tree is on each of the side seams. The lid is circled with linked Indian good luck symbols. One of these symbols also appears on the lid knob.

∾————**Lovebirds Butter Holder**————∾

The pair of lovebirds appears on both sides of this butter holder which is unique for the pattern because the flying birds motif is incorporated with the lovebirds on some forms such as salt holders, cookie jars, and the Flying Birds pitcher.

SIZE: 5½"h, 6"w
AVAILABILITY: Extremely rare
COLORS: Blue and white
MINT VALUE: $500.00 – $600.00

A band of very delicate flowers accents the top and bottom edges of the crock as well as the top of the lid and its sides. The bail on the example above is a replacement. The lovebirds pattern on the example at left is so clear that the feathers on the birds can be seen.

∾————**Open Rose Pastry Crock**————∾

Open roses highlighted in diffused blue accent a white waffle background on the sides of this pastry crock. The waffle pattern is repeated on the lid with a thin unglazed ring separating waffle bands. A butter holder in the Open Rose pattern was also produced but is not shown.

Butter Holder (not shown)
SIZE: 4½"h, 6"w
AVAILABILITY: Rare pattern
COLORS: Blue and white
MINT VALUE: $250.00 – $300.00

Pastry Crock
SIZE: 5"h, 7½"w
AVAILABILITY: Rare pattern
COLORS: Blue and white
MINT VALUE: $400.00 – $450.00

Pansies Butter Holder

SIZE: 4"h, 6"w
AVAILABILITY: Extremely rare
COLORS: Green and cream
MINT VALUE: $400.00 – $450.00

Four framed panels of pansies separated by a diamond lattice background pattern surround the crock. A chain link border encircles the top edge of the crock. The lid is especially notable due to its unique handle. Instead of a knob, which is most common, an applied lift handle has been added. Although faint, pansies in four groupings show on the lid. The same border which surrounds the panels of pansies is repeated around the lid's edge.

Peacock Butter Holder

SIZE: 6"h, 6"w
AVAILABILITY: Extremely rare
COLORS: Blue and white
MINT VALUE: $500.00 – $600.00

The peacock gracefully strolls on a brick path bordered by an urn and palm trees. "Butter" is stenciled on a front plate obviously made in the mold for that purpose. The elegant lipped lid is edged with a band of pearl beading on the side and groupings of swaying palm trees on the top. A palm tree top also embellishes the knob. An unglazed band surrounds the outside edge of the lid.

Printed Cows Butter Holder

SIZE: 5"h, 6½"w
AVAILABILITY: Common
COLORS: White with blue stenciling
MINT VALUE: $150.00 – $175.00 (with lid and bail)

The stenciled grazing cow scene appears on one side only between two blue bands. This example is missing its original lid. Bail attachment holes are pierced into each side of the rim.

Reverse Pyramids and Columns Pastry Crock

SIZE: 5"h, 7½"w
AVAILABILITY: Scarce
COLORS: Blue and white
MINT VALUE: $175.00 – $225.00

A band of reverse pyramids around the top rim overlays columns surrounding the base of this simple pastry crock. The bail has been replaced and the original lid is missing from this example.

Swastika Butter Holder

SIZE: 5½"h, 7½"w
AVAILABILITY: Scarce
COLORS: Blue and white
MINT VALUE: $250.00 – $300.00

Although faint, the word "BUTTER" is centered on an orange peel background and is flanked on each side with a large swastika symbol which is also known as the Indian good luck sign.

Smaller swastika symbols circle the top rim and base as well as the outside edge of the lid. A plain white area of orange peel pattern is separated from the blue outside swastika ring on the lid by a narrow, unglazed band.

Stenciled and Advertising Butter Holders

	Lambrecht Butter	Kaukauna Klub Crock	Stonehill's Butter
SIZE:	3"h, 4¾"w	4¾"h, 5½"w	4"h, 6¼"w
AVAILABILITY:	Scarce	Common	Scarce
COLORS:	Blue and white	Blue and white	Blue and white
MINT VALUE:	$45.00 – $65.00	$45.00 – $65.00	$65.00 – $75.00

These advertising butter holders were probably returnable containers which were refilled by the producer and delivered to homes in the same manner as milk. The Kaukauna Klub example is seen in a variety of sizes with this example most likely being a cheese crock.

SIZE: 4"h, 9"w
AVAILABILITY: Scarce
COLORS: Blue and white
MINT VALUE: $250.00 – $275.00

An intricately designed pattern provides a frame for "Butter" which is stenciled on one side only. Two blue bands accent the top and bottom of the crock. The large lid nestles into a rim shelf.

A stenciled butter labeling is accented with bands of diffused blue around the top and bottom of these quantity butter holders which were produced in several sizes. The lids fit into recessed rims. Because of the container's size and the weight of its contents when filled, the bail attachment for the two larger sizes is different from the smaller example. The lids and bails are original on all the examples shown.

Stenciled Butters:

	Small (bottom right)	Medium (top left)	Large (bottom left)
SIZE:	4½"h, 6"w	5½"h, 6"w	7"h, 7"w
AVAILABILITY:	Scarce	Scarce	Scarce
COLORS:	Blue and white	Blue and white	Blue and white
MINT VALUE:	$200.00 – $250.00	$200.00 – $250.00	$250.00 – $300.00

Both sides of this sponged butter holder from the Village Farm Dairy are shown above. This example was probably a returnable container which was refilled by the dairy and delivered to the homes it served.

Sponged and Stenciled Butters:

	Sponge (above)	Large Stenciled (below left)	Small Stenciled (below right)
SIZE:	4"h, 5½"w	5½"h, 6"w	7"h, 7"w
AVAILABILITY:	Scarce	Scarce	Scarce
COLORS:	Blue and white	Blue and white	Blue and white
MINT VALUE:	$125.00 – $150.00	$145.00 – $175.00	$145.00 – $175.00

Two butter holders with dark blue stenciling are shown below.
The original lids are missing, and the bails are replacements.

Section V – Salt Holders

Salt holders, as the name implies, held loose, coarse salt. The holder was kept inside a kitchen cabinet or hung on the kitchen wall, the flat back plate nailed securely to the wall.

A "pinch" of salt could easily be obtained from the holder. With frequent use in this era, salt holder lids were often broken, chipped, or lost entirely. Salt holders were produced in a variety of patterns making it possible to coordinate the same pattern throughout a kitchen. For example, such common patterns as the Apricot can be seen in salt holders, pitchers, bowls, butter holders, and crocks.

The Peacock was also a popular pattern which could be coordinated throughout the kitchen. In addition to salt holders, the Peacock pattern was produced on pitchers, bowls, butter crocks, custard cups, and coffee pots.

Apple Blossom

The word "SALT" is highlighted in dark blue on the front of this piece. On the sides are apple blossom flowers, stems, and leaves. On each side of the flat back plate are two shell-like decorations. The background is a diamond-shaped waffle pattern. The lid is extremely detailed with apple blossom flowers and leaves.

SIZE:	5"h (front), 6½"h (back); 6"w (bottom)
AVAILABILITY:	Extremely rare
COLORS:	Blue and white
MINT VALUE:	$200.00 – $250.00 without lid; $350.00 – $425.00 with lid

Apricot with Honeycomb

SIZE: 4"h (front), 6"h (back), 6"w (base)
AVAILABILITY: Common
COLORS: Blue and white, rarely seen in green and cream
MINT VALUE: $100.00 – $150.00 without lid; $175.00 – $225.00 with lid

The Apricot with Honeycomb pattern was commonly used on salt holders, pitchers, and butter crocks. While the example shown has lighter blue coloration, a wide range of coloring can be seen from light to dark blues. Note that the "SALT" lettering has been left white on this example and has not been highlighted. A cluster of apricots appears on each side of the word "SALT" with the background being a honeycomb texture. While the holder in this example is in excellent condition, the lid is missing, reducing its value. The original lid for this salt holder is similar to the lid for the Apricot with Honeycomb covered bowl on page 153.

Blackberry

The Blackberry salt holder is a simple but utilitarian piece. The "SALT" letters are in very dark blue on this example. Blackberries in a cluster extend on each side of the lettering into the side seams. The smooth background surface is given depth by the bands of diffused blue around the top and bottom.

Simple form and coloring characterize the Blackberry pattern salt holder. Overall lighter blue diffusing makes this example quite different from the one shown above. The coloring is almost solid blue with diffusing much lighter around the word "SALT." The distinct pattern of blackberries can be seen in the photo on the right which provides a view from the side. While the holder itself is in excellent condition, it is missing its original lid which does reduce its value. The Blackberry pattern appears to have been used predominantly on salt holders.

SIZE: 4½"h (front), 6"w (bottom)
AVAILABILITY: Common
COLORS: Blue and white
MINT VALUE: $150.00 – $175.00 without lid;
$250.00 – $275.00 with lid

Butterfly

Using the standard orange peel background typical of the Butterfly pattern, the design of the salt crock is quite simple. Four butterflies with open wings surround the crock. Vertical ribbing provides the base for blue diffused borders around the top and bottom rims. A missing original lid in this example has been replaced by a wooden one.

SIZE: 4¼"h (front), 6"h (back), 6"w (bottom)
AVAILABILITY: Scarce pattern
COLORS: Blue and white only
MINT VALUE: $150.00 – $175.00 without lid; $250.00 – $275.00 with lid

Daisy on Snowflake

Vertical, horizontal, and diagonal mold lines provide a delicate snowflake style background. Daisies surround the crock base at intervals. The pattern is repeated on the matching original lid. Vertical ribbing around the top and bottom rims provides the base for diffused blue borders. The "SALT" lettering is highlighted in dark blue on most examples seen.

SIZE: 4¼"h (front), 6"h (back), 6"w (bottom); lid, 5¼"w
AVAILABILITY: Common pattern
COLORS: Blue and white only
MINT VALUE: $150.00 – $175.00 without lid; $250.00 – $275.00 with lid

Notice the flat, buttonlike lid knob on the example at left. The Daisy on Snowflake pattern appears to have been used only on salt crocks; the pattern has not been seen on other types of pieces.

Eagle

SIZE: 4¼"h (front), 6"h (back), 5½"w (bottom)
AVAILABILITY: Extremely rare pattern
COLORS: Blue and white only
MINT VALUE: $250.00 – $325.00 without lid; $425.00 – $575.00 with lid

    Whether on a pitcher, salt holder, or butter crock, the Eagle pattern is highly desirable because of its rarity and intricate design. The impressed dots pattern with roping and scrolling serves as a classic setting for the majestic eagle in flight clutching a shield and arrows. Eagles on either side of "SALT" on the front of the crock are flying in the same direction. Only the background pattern is presented on the back side of the crock as well as on original lids. Less than distinct mold pattern, lighter blue coloration, and no highlighting on "SALT," as well as a missing original lid, serve as examples of factors which reduce the value of a piece, such as in the examples shown in the two bottom photos.

Grapes on Basketweave

SIZE: 4"h (front), 5¾"w (bottom)
AVAILABILITY: Rare pattern, not commonly seen
COLORS: Blue and white only
MINT VALUE: $125.00 – $175.00 without lid; $175.00 – $225.00 with lid

A small cluster of grapes and a leaf are on both sides of the "SALT" notation. The background is a basketweave pattern. With a crack and some small chips in the front and the original lid missing, this example, by definition, is considered to be in fair condition, thus affecting its actual market value.

Grapevine on Fence

SIZE: 4½"h (front), 6"w (bottom)
AVAILABILITY: Rare pattern
COLORS: Blue and white only
MINT VALUE: $175.00 – $225.00 without lid; $275.00 – $300.00 with lid

This salt features a cluster of grapes in the front center over a stenciled "SALT." The sides and back of the holder have a fence and lattice pattern. The original lid is missing.

Greek Key

SIZE: 4½"h, 5½"w; lid, 4½"w
AVAILABILITY: Extremely rare pattern
COLORS: Blue and white
MINT VALUE: $125.00 – $175.00 without lid; $175.00 – $225.00 with lid

"SALT" is stenciled on only one side in large Old English letters and flanked by two small oak leaves. The matching lid sits in an inside groove and distinctly shows the Greek Key motif. Note that this is a free-standing salt container and does not have the wall hanging option of many other salts.

Lovebirds

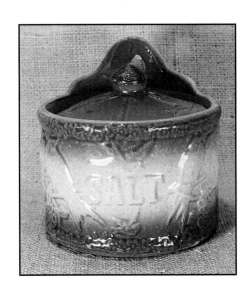 

SIZE: 4¼"h (front), 6"h (back), 6"w (bottom)
AVAILABILITY: Rare pattern, not commonly seen
COLORS: Blue and white only
MINT VALUE: $225.00 – $275.00 without lid; $350.00 – $450.00 with lid

Diffused blue bands at top and bottom frame the bird motif on this salt holder. The lovebirds design is used on either side of "SALT" in the front while the birds in flight design graces the back side of the crock. Note that "SALT" on this example is not highlighted in blue as on many pieces. The original lid repeats the birds in flight design.

As shown to the left, the flying birds theme is presented on the back side of the Lovebirds salt holder in the same manner as on the lid. The knob on the lid is also more pronounced than seen on some salt holders. This lid is raised and almost appears to be in a roof-like shape versus flat lids seen on other salt holders. Another example with a replacement wooden lid is shown below.

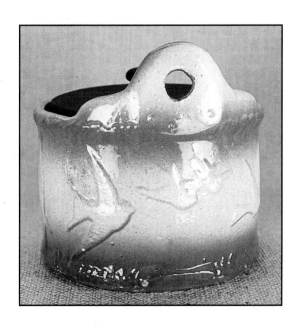

Lovebirds (Reproduction)

SIZE: 4"h (front), 5¾"h (back), 5½"w (bottom)
AVAILABILITY: Reproduction
COLORS: Blue and white only
REPRO VALUE: $30.00

Hopefully, it is obvious that this example is a reproduction as compared to the Lovebirds salt holders presented on the previous two pages. This example is presented for comparison and educational purposes so that one may be in a better position of recognizing the many molded stoneware reproductions which are on the market but which are not always marked as such by the seller. Notice that the blue is quite different from the older pieces and that the white areas are really "white." Notice also that the lid does not have the flying bird design as original lids do.

Peacock

SIZE: 4½"h (front), 6"h (back), 6"w (bottom); lid, 5¼"w
AVAILABILITY: Extremely rare pattern
COLORS: Blue and white
MINT VALUE: $325.00 – $375.00 without lid; $450.00 – $550.00 with lid

The peacock appears at the front center surrounded by urns, columns, and palm trees while the "SALT" lettering is stenciled below in dark blue. The bottom band is a brick path, and the top band is accented with a string of pearl beading. The lid features a peacock on each side encircled by the pearl beading. The peacock series always appears in very light blues.

This Peacock salt holder has one of the deepest, clearest patterns which has been seen. The lid shown above is obviously not an original Peacock pattern; however, it may well have been original to this holder as the spoke motif could have been a generic lid which was usable with various patterns.

Rickrack on Waffle

SIZE: 4½"h (front), 6"w (bottom)
AVAILABILITY: Rare pattern
COLORS: Blue and white
MINT VALUE: $150.00 – $200.00 without lid; $275.00 – $325.00 with lid

Bands of rickrack surround the top and bottom on the salt holder as well as encircle the lid of this example which features a waffle background. Smaller-sized block style lettering on the front is highlighted in dark blue.

Stenciled

This stenciled salt holder once had a hinged, wooden lid. Note the old rusty screw near the center of the back plate. This piece contains heavy stenciling on all sides. It is possible that the piece is not American since many European pieces had hinged wooden lids. As well, the bottom has an interesting texture which is like puffed rice.

SIZE: 4"h (front), 4¼"w (bottom)
AVAILABILITY: Scarce pattern
COLORS: Blue and white
MINT VALUE: $125.00 – $175.00 without lid; $175.00 – $225.00 with lid

SIZE: 4¾"h (front), 5¾"w (bottom)
AVAILABILITY: Scarce pattern
COLORS: Blue and white
MINT VALUE: $125.00 – $175.00 without lid; $175.00 – $225.00 with lid

This stenciled salt is decorated with an array of patterns. It almost appears that the maker used whatever could be found due to all the variations. Notice that the "SALT" lettering is different from the example above and also notice the pattern differences. The hinged, wooden lid is a replacement.

Waffle

SIZE: 4"h (front), 6"w (bottom)
AVAILABILITY: Common
COLORS: Blue and white
MINT VALUE: $125.00 – $175.00 without lid;
             $175.00 – $225.00 with lid

This very simple pattern has a waffle background with "SALT" in large block lettering highlighted in dark blue. The original lid is missing.

Section VI – Rolling Pins

Rolling pins are one of the most beautiful pieces of a collection. It is hard to believe that something that is so valuable now was once given away free, somewhat like you get a free toaster with a new bank account today! It is likely that some "rollers," as they are often called, were sold, but they were commonly given away as premiums and promotional items. They were sometimes packed inside sacks of flour or simply given to a patron with a sale. The term "advertiser" is given to ones with a message on one or both sides. An advertiser with a message on both sides is considered to be more rare than one with a message appearing on only one side. Most stenciled messages include some reference as to what the store sold, such as "dry goods," or a reference to its service, such as "undertaking." A very few messages make reference to a city and state location of the business. Most advertisers use the "stenciled wildflower" pattern which appears on both ends usually in concert with blue band accents.

One of the rarest rollers is the swirl. The swirls are sometimes counted although that number does not really contribute to the overall value of a roller. Condition, color clarity, presence of promotional message, and overall appeal is a better determination of value for rollers.

Rollers were produced in basically two sizes, large and small. The five basic patterns seen are:
1. plain wildflowers
2. advertiser wildflowers
3. banded
4. banded advertisers
5. swirl

Although the banded rollers are seen in shades of blue and sometimes orange or green, the wildflower patterns and the swirls have blue accenting on white pottery and are never seen in other colors.

Patterns were often used on multiple utilitarian pieces such as the Dutch Boy and Girl pattern on this extremely rare rolling pin, the milk pitcher, and the mug. Collecting groupings in the same pattern can be quite challenging but most rewarding for the collector when accomplished.

Dutch Boy and Girl

SIZE: Roller 8"l, 3"d; 14½"l with handles
AVAILABILITY: Extremely rare pattern
COLORS: Blue and white
MINT VALUE: $2,500.00 – $3,000.00+

The Dutch Boy and Girl scene with a windmill in the background appears between bold blue lines. The design is repeated on the opposite side. Between the two scenes is a fern-like leaf decoration shown in the photo at right. The surface is totally decorated with little open space. The maple handles are perfect. This is quite possibly a one-of-a-kind item.

Swirl

The swirls of diffused blues go around the roller at an angle. The maple handles are original. The swirl pattern is seen on coffee and tea pots and Boston baked beans crocks as well.

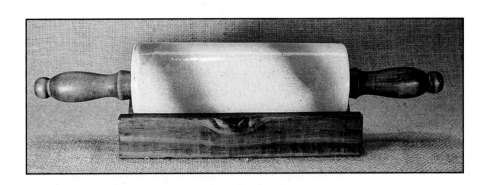

SIZE: Roller 7¼"l, 2½"d; 15"l
with handles
AVAILABILITY: Rare pattern
COLORS: Blue and white
MINT VALUE: $800.00 – $1,000.00+

~ Swirl — Baker's Size ~

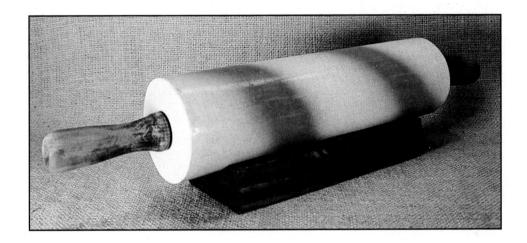

SIZE: Roller 10"l, 3"d; 16"l with handles
AVAILABILITY: Extremely rare size
COLORS: Blue and white (almost turquoise blue)
MINT VALUE: $1,200.00 – $1,500.00

This is a baker's size in the rare Swirl pattern. The color is interesting in that the blue is not what is normally seen. Note the size difference by comparing the standard-sized roller in the photo below showing both rollers.

Swirl with Star

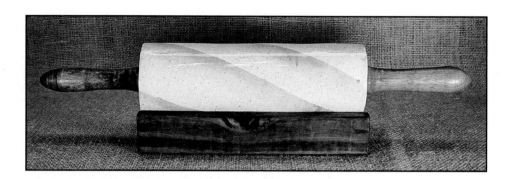

SIZE: Roller 9"l, 3"d; 17"l with handles
AVAILABILITY: Extremely rare size and pattern
COLORS: Blue and white
MINT VALUE: $1,200.00 – $1,500.00

This Swirl roller has an extra bonus of a star pattern on each end where the handle is attached. This roller is longer than most others with generous handles as well.

Wildflower (with center decoration)

SIZE: Roller 7¼"l, 2½"d; 15"l with handles
AVAILABILITY: Rare pattern
COLORS: Blue and white
MINT VALUE: $500.00 – $600.00

The center flower decoration makes this Wildflower roller quite special. The flower also appears on the other side. When this roller was purchased, the handles were painted mint green; perhaps the original owner wanted a change. They have since been stripped of the green paint and waxed to a nice finish.

Wildflower (dark stenciling)

SIZE: Roller 8"l, 3"d; 16½"l
with handles
AVAILABILITY: Common
COLORS: Blue and white
MINT VALUE: $350.00 – $450.00

The example at left shows nice dark blue decoration on a roller with the Wildflower stenciled pattern. The wooden handles are unusual.

Wildflower Rollers

Several examples of Wildflower rollers are presented below. Note that the bands are recessed from the ends of the roller in the top photo as compared with other Wildflower examples. The rollers in the bottom two photos are smaller-sized rollers. Pottery rollers often acquired a variety of handle styles as is obvious with the examples presented. The handles in the bottom photo are attached to a wooden shaft with a metal pin as can be seen on the left handle of the roller.

SIZE: Roller 8"l, 3"d; 16½"l
with handles
AVAILABILITY: Common
COLORS: Blue and white
MINT VALUE: $350.00 – $450.00

SIZE: Roller 7½"l, 2¾"d; 14"l
with handles
AVAILABILITY: Common
COLORS: Blue and white
MINT VALUE: $275.00 – $375.00

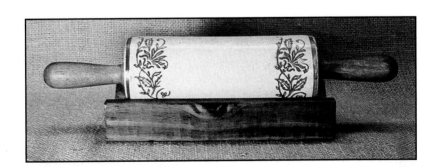

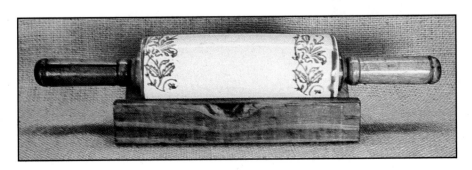

SIZE: Roller 7½"l, 2¾"d; 14"l
with handles
AVAILABILITY: Common
COLORS: Blue and white
MINT VALUE: $275.00 – $375.00

—Wildflower (larger size)—

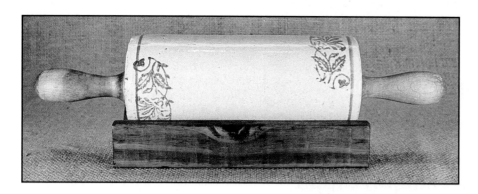

This is a larger-sized light blue Wildflower stenciled roller. Since it does have some end flakes and chips, it is considered to be in Good condition thus affecting its market value. The handle simply slips on a center rod as is shown below with the roller and handles disassembled. While Wildflower rollers are rated common in comparison to other roller patterns, they can still command quite high market prices.

SIZE: Roller 8"l, 3"d; 15"l
      with handles
AVAILABILITY: Common
COLORS: Blue and white
MINT VALUE: $350.00 – $450.00

—Wildflower Rollers with Advertising—

Several examples of Wildflower rollers with advertising are presented below and on the next three pages. Merchants were keenly aware of the power of having their names, literally, in front of potential customers during the everyday tasks which they performed. From dry goods to furniture to undertaking, merchants often used these rollers as giveaway premiums to promote their businesses.

SIZE: Roller 8"l, 3"d; 14½"l with handles
AVAILABILITY: Rare with city and state identified
COLORS: Blue and white
MINT VALUE: $450.00 – $500.00

This roller does have a light pattern and some roughness which would decrease its value; however, its slogan is quite unique which would likely allow a less-than-mint example to retain more value: "Compliments of/Reams, Jones & Blankenship/Roanoke, VA/MARRY THE GIRL/We'll furnish the home."

This particular roller was among 20 or so just like it which were discovered in an old general store in Ohio. While many collectors thought them to be reproductions, it seems they are uniquely American. Unlike other advertisers, these were made for a Russian immigrant family who ran a store in America. The writing is thought to be Ukrainian with the message appearing on both sides of the roller.

Above: SIZE: Roller 7¾"l, 3"d; 13½"l with handles
AVAILABILITY: Rare with double printed sides and origin
COLORS: Blue and white
MINT VALUE: $500.00 – $600.00

Right: SIZE: Roller 8"l, 3"d; 14½"l with handles
AVAILABILITY: Rare with combination advertising
COLORS: Blue and white
MINT VALUE: $450.00 – $500.00

This roller demonstrates the unique combinations of businesses that once existed: The Ball and Harris Furniture Company/Furniture and Undertaking/"THE STORE THAT SATISFIES."

The printing "BEST GOODS, LOWEST PRICES/SAMUEL F. ERWIN." on this roller provides a classic example of an advertising roller probably given as a premium by this merchant for which there is no known location. This smaller-sized roller with the same message on the reverse side has excellent coloration and form. The bottom left photo shows the assembly of the original handles. The arched top line of the message is also an attractive feature of this example.

SIZE: Roller 7½"l, 3"d; 15"l
with handles
AVAILABILITY: Rare with double
printed sides
COLORS: Blue and white
MINT VALUE: $500.00 – $600.00

SIZE: Roller 7½"l, 3"d; 15"l with handles
AVAILABILITY: Scarce
COLORS: Blue and white
MINT VALUE: $450.00 – $500.00

The simple message "COMPLIMENTS/A. E. RENNER" enhances this Wildflower roller which has excellent coloration and symmetry.

SIZE: Roller 8"l, 3"d; 14½"l
with handles
AVAILABILITY: Scarce
COLORS: Blue and white
MINT VALUE: $450.00 – $500.00

A larger-sized merchant advertising roller labeled "Your Trade is Appreciated at/The Ruff Gussman Co./'NEW STORE'" was possibly given as a token to customers to celebrate its grand opening. The message appears on one side only; the light-colored handles are original.

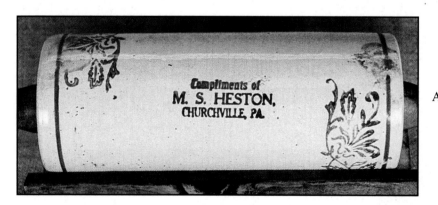

SIZE: Roller 7½"l, 3"d; 15"l with handles
AVAILABILITY: Rare with city and state identified
COLORS: Blue and white
MINT VALUE: $450.00 – $500.00

"Compliments of/M. S. HESTON,/CHURCHVILLE, PA." provides the message which this merchant wished to remind the "biscuit maker" of each morning. The wildflower stenciling on each end of this example is offset which is more typical than symmetrical examples. Note the smeared blue on the right end, a fairly common indicator of mass production.

SIZE: Roller 8"l, 3"d; 14½"l with handles
AVAILABILITY: Rare with city and state identified
COLORS: Blue and white
MINT VALUE: $500.00 – $600.00

"Compliments of McFALL & WARN/E. STROUDSBURG, PA." Several factors make this a very unique roller including its large size, mint condition, original handles, dark coloration, very large one-half inch letters, and the identification of a specific city and state. The handle assembly in the photo at right shows the unique screw-on feature of the center rod.

∽——Wildflower Rollers with Advertising — Baker's Size——∾

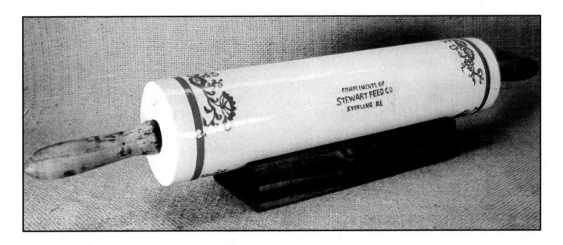

SIZE: Roller 10"l, 3"d; 16"l with handles
AVAILABILITY: Rare size with city and state identified
COLORS: Blue and white
MINT VALUE: $1,200.00 – $1,500.00

This rare roller has two important attributes. First, the advertiser is identified by city and state. Second, it is in a very rare baker's size. The message "Compliments of/STEWART FEED CO/Sterling, Ill." indicates that it was probably a premium given by a feed store which is, in itself, an unusual feature. The end, as noted at left, carries a maker's mark which appears to be two crossed swords. Note also that the flower decoration is different from other Wildflower rollers commonly seen.

Banded Rollers

This roller has triple bands of rust color on each end. One wide band is highlighted by a thinner line on each side. Even plain banded versions of rollers are not frequently seen.

SIZE: Roller 8"l, 3"d; 15½"l with handles
AVAILABILITY: Scarce color
COLORS: Rust and white shown; also in dark blue and white
MINT VALUE: $350.00 – $450.00

This triple-banded roller has an unusually large number of advertising lines. Note the variations in both the size and style of the lettering which appears on one side only. The two-color combination with rust bands and blue lettering also adds to the attractiveness of this example. "COMPLIMENTS OF/POSTVILLE VARIETY STORE,/J. H. DANNENBRINK, Prop./SOMETHING FOR EVERYONE/*QUALITY FIRST*."

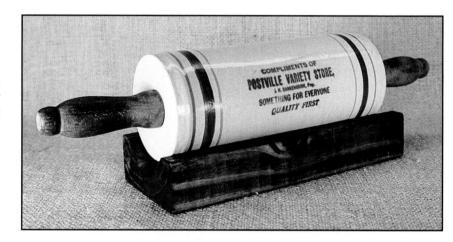

SIZE: Roller 8"l, 3"d; 14½"l with handles
AVAILABILITY: Rare pattern and color combination
COLORS: Rust, blue and white
MINT VALUE: $550.00 – $650.00

Another example of a triple-banded roller with an unusually large number of advertising lines is shown at left. The unique message, as well as the inclusion of the phone number, makes this a prime example of a banded advertising roller. The message appears on one side only with the bands in rust and the lettering in dark blue. "TO KNEAD GOOD BREAD/YOU NEED GOOD FLOUR/FOR THE BEST COME TO/J. B. DAKIN/PHONE 1, SCHALLER, IOWA."

SIZE: Roller 8"l, 3"d; 14½"l with handles
AVAILABILITY: Rare pattern with city and state identification and color combination
COLORS: Rust, blue and white
MINT VALUE: $550.00 – $650.00

SIZE: Roller 8"l, 3"d; 14¾"l with handles
AVAILABILITY: Rare pattern and color combination
COLORS: Rust, blue and white
MINT VALUE: $550.00 – $650.00

The combination of the large, dark navy lettering and rust triple bands is a unique feature of this roller. With an uncommon two-color combination, this roller is enhanced further by its catchy slogan and maple handles. The advertising appears on one side only: BUY AT/CAPPEL'S/AND SAVE "DOUGH."

A plain blue banded roller is transformed into a wealth of information about this merchant with the printed message "Pahde Bros./FARMERS EXCHANGE/Dealers in General Merchandise/PHONE 183 J. — EAST MAIN STREET/MT. OLIVE, ILLINOIS." The simple dark blue and white coloration strikingly frames the message.

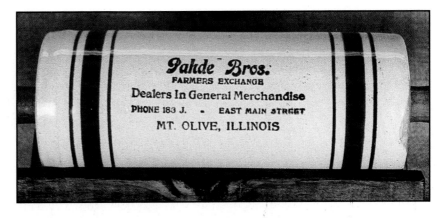

SIZE: Roller 8"l, 3"d; 14½"l with handles
AVAILABILITY: Rare pattern with city and state identification and rare color
COLORS: Dark blue and white
MINT VALUE: $550.00 – $650.00

∽——Yellow Ware Roller——∽

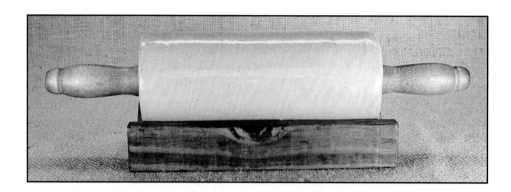

SIZE: Roller 8"l, 3"d; 15"l with handles
AVAILABILITY: Scarce
COLORS: Yellow ware
MINT VALUE: $350.00 – $450.00

Any collection of stoneware rolling pins would be incomplete without one in yellow ware. The two examples shown are differentiated only by the types of handles which were attached.

While yellow ware is certainly a type of collectible pottery unto itself, the grouping below indicates that molds such as the Grazing Cows pattern found themselves filled with a variety of clays and finished with a variety of glazes. It is possible that many of the mold patterns were produced in yellow ware, although most would be considered quite rare. Lovebirds pitchers as well as Spear Point and Flower Panels measuring cups were known to have been produced in yellow ware also.

Section VII – Bowls and Crocks

For antiques enthusiasts, the stainless steel, plastic, and glass bowls commonly used today simply lack the character and nostalgia of those used in earlier times. Stoneware bowls were actually a welcomed invention for grandmother, replacing wooden containers which were often the mainstay mixing vessel.

Stoneware bowls were produced in a variety of patterns with graduated diameter sizes from as small as 4 inches to larger than 13 inches. "Nesting sets" allowed compact storage as well as the convenience of selecting the right size for the task, whether separating eggs for making meringue for a pie, or mixing a family-sized batch of biscuits.

Because of its tolerance to heat, stoneware was also molded in a bowl form and equipped with a wooden handle wire bail for stovetop use. These flat-bottomed crocks with grooves and ridges for heat circulation were used for stewing and warming contents on top of wood-fired cookstoves. With the handy bail, the crock could go easily from the stovetop to the table, serving both utilitarian and decorative function.

Known also as bail bowls and stovetop pieces, these versatile bowls are commonly called milk crocks. The larger bailed versions, especially, could hold a quantity of milk for clabbering, hence the name Milk Crock with Bail used in this section. Filled with fresh milk, covered with a cloth, and placed in a warm spot near the cookstove, the crock would provide clabbered milk to be churned into fresh butter for the next meal.

Bowls and crocks were also used for food storage. Most have "collars" over which a cloth cover could be placed and secured with a piece of string. Few were produced with matching lids.

A complete nesting set of Scrolled Band bowls in green and cream, as shown below, usually consisted of eight different sizes which would meet the needs of almost any kitchen.

Apple Blossom on Trellis Milk Crock with Bail

SIZE: 5¼"h, 10½"w (across top)
AVAILABILITY: Scarce pattern
COLORS: Blue and white
MINT VALUE: $200.00 – $250.00

A single apple blossom in blue diffusing adorns four sides of this milk crock. The lattice-pattern background below the bowl's collar is accented by the solid blue collar which has a repeating scalloped pattern of incised lines. The wire bail is a replacement.

The bottom of the Apple Blossom on Trellis milk crock shown at right is ribbed, with the word "PATENTED" molded in the center and a faint cross trademark.

Apple Blossom on Trellis Bowl

This Apple Blossom on Trellis bowl shown below may have been used for a variety of purposes including mixing and holding smaller quantities of milk for clabbering prior to churning. The pattern is the same as on the bail version.

A single apple blossom in blue diffusing adorns four sides of this bowl. The lattice-pattern background below the bowl's collar is accented by the solid blue collar which has a repeating scalloped pattern of incised lines. The Apple Blossom on Trellis bowl was also produced in a rare smaller size, 2½" high, 7½" wide, with its value being 25 percent higher than the larger size.

SIZE: 3¾"h, 9¼"w (across top)
AVAILABILITY: Scarce pattern
COLORS: Blue and white
MINT VALUE: $125.00 – $150.00

The milk crock with bail is also referred to as a bail bowl and a stovetop piece. With the handy bail, the crock could go easily from the stove to the table. A rare smaller version of the Apple Blossom on Trellis Milk Crock with Bail is presented at right with the bottom shown in the photo at the bottom of the previous page.

SIZE:	4"h, 8½"w (across top)
AVAILABILITY:	Scarce pattern, extremely rare size
COLORS:	Blue and white
MINT VALUE:	$250.00 – $300.00

Apricot with Honeycomb Bowl

Examples of the Apricot with Honeycomb pattern bowl in each of the three color combinations in which it was produced are shown here and on the next page. The blue and white, and green and cream colors are the most common while the blue and tan shown below is seen occasionally.

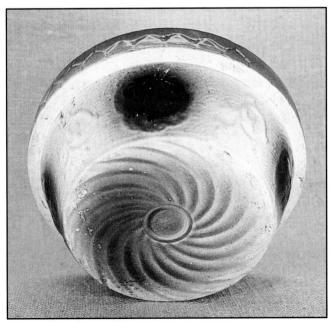

REGULAR SIZE:	4"h, 9¼"w (across top)
AVAILABILITY:	Common pattern
COLORS:	Blue and white, green and cream, blue and tan
MINT VALUE:	$95.00 – $125.00
SMALL SIZE:	2½"h, 7½"w (across top) (see next page, bottom right)
AVAILABILITY:	Common pattern, extremely rare size
COLORS:	Green and cream (only known colors in this size)
MINT VALUE:	$150.00 – $200.00

The apricots appear four times around the bowl with a honeycomb design between each. The rim has a chickenwire effect and typically has diffused color around the apricot clusters.

The bottom of each of these crocks has an interesting swirl design which seems to be unique to this pattern. The top and bottom of the collar rim are typically not glazed.

The regular (or larger) size Apricot with Honeycomb bowl is commonly found in green and blue. The small size seen here is quite rare. The comparison at left shows a rare smaller size next to a standard size example.

⌒——— Apricot with Honeycomb Covered Bowl———⌒

SIZE: 4"h, 9¼"w (across top, bowl only)
AVAILABILITY: Common pattern, set is rare
COLORS: Blue and white
MINT VALUE: $400.00 – $450.00

While the Apricot with Honeycomb bowl is commonly found, it is extremely rare to complete the set with a lid. The lid repeats the design of the bowl with apricots appearing in four circles around a center knob. The rim design of the bowl is repeated around the outer edge of the lid. The lid has an interior self rim that seats it securely on the bowl.

⌒———Apricot with Honeycomb Milk Crock with Bail———⌒

The dark blue coloration and original bail add to the value of this example. The pattern is also very distinct. The apricot pattern is the same as on the bowl, only somewhat enlarged on the bailed version.

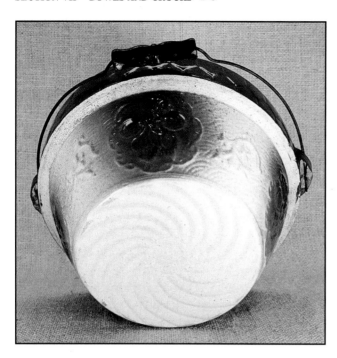

LARGE SIZE: 5¼"h, 10½"w (across top)
AVAILABILITY: Common pattern
COLORS: Blue and white, green and cream
MINT VALUE: $175.00 – $225.00

SMALL SIZE: 4"h, 8½"w (across top)
AVAILABILITY: Common pattern, extremely rare size
COLORS: Blue and white, green and cream
MINT VALUE: $200.00 – $250.00

This green example at right of an Apricot with Honeycomb bail bowl has very good deep green color. Some of these are very light green as the rim color of this one shows. It is the same size and value as seen in blue above.

The interesting handle attachment is shown at left. Most bail bowls have only one hole through which the attachment wire goes while this example has two holes. The pattern on this example is very deeply molded.

The smaller-sized milk crock (right) is especially noticeable when compared to the larger one. While availability is rated as common, bail bowls are becoming increasingly difficult to find in good condition. All of these examples have replaced bails.

Basketweave Cereal Bowl

SIZE: 2¼"h, 5"w (across top)
AVAILABILITY: Rare pattern
COLORS: Blue and white
MINT VALUE: $125.00 – $150.00

This simple cereal bowl has the basketweave pattern on all sides with a roped rim. The top is medium blue which fades to an all white bottom.

——Clothespins Milk Crock with Bail——

SIZE: 5"h, 10"w (across top)
AVAILABILITY: Rare pattern
COLORS: Light blue
MINT VALUE: $200.00 – $225.00

This Clothespins Milk Crock with Bail apparently served its purpose quite well as is evident from the wear on the bottom. The vertical markings around the crock closely resemble old-fashioned clothespins. Notice the large star (maker's mark) molded in the bottom center and circled along the edge with a bank of short ribbing for heat circulation.

——Cosmos Bowls——

A small version of the Cosmos bowl is shown at left. The pattern on this bowl, though faint, is the same as on the larger one on the facing page. This small size is extremely rare. As with many crockery bowls, the Cosmos pattern was probably produced in a nesting set of four to six bowls. While a complete nesting set was not available for photographing, if one were found, its value for the complete set could be estimated at $1,500.00.

SIZES: 4¾"h, 9¾"w (for large bowl)
2½"h, 4¾"w (for small bowl, facing page)
AVAILABILITY: Rare pattern
COLORS: Blue and white
MINT VALUES: $150.00 – $175.00 (small bowl)
$225.00 – $250.00 (large bowl)

Cosmos flowers framed by beading appear at intervals around the sides. The waffle background is accented by a ribbed collar in solid blue. The example at left and above has brilliant color and deeply cut pattern marks.

Currants and Diamonds Bowl

SIZE: 5"h, 10"w; Bottom, 5¼"w
AVAILABILITY: Rare pattern
COLORS: Blue and white
MINT VALUE: $175.00 – $225.00

The Currants and Diamonds bowl has an exquisite pattern unlike that found on any other item of molded stoneware. The pattern was apparently used solely on bowls. The deeply molded geometric diamond background is accentuated by four clusters of blue-highlighted currants around the bowl.

Custard Cups

Custards in any pattern are not easy to find. Since sets are a real rarity, a matched set of six may command $1,000.00 to $1,200.00. At left is shown the popular fishscale pattern, a sponged example, and a stenciled example.

At center left and bottom left are two sizes of the Scrolls pattern to demonstrate the size variations which were not unusual in mass-produced molded stoneware. Also at bottom left is a Grapes on Trellis custard cup in the foreground. Above is another example of a Fishscale cup with different coloration. Later in this section is a Peacock custard cup which is shown with the Peacock bowls.

SIZE: 2½ – 3"h, 3" – 4"w (varies from cup to cup)
                (most common 2½" h, 3"w)
AVAILABILITY: Rare in any pattern
COLORS: Blue and white, stenciled, sponge
MINT VALUE: $125.00 – $150.00

⌒——Daisy and Lattice Milk Crock with Bail——⌒

SIZE: 5"h, 10"w; Bottom, 6"w
AVAILABILITY: Common pattern
COLORS: Blue and white
MINT VALUE: $200.00 – $250.00

The daisy appears on a lattice background one time on each side in the center of the crock. Notice that the vertical slats of the latticework are double, whereas the horizontal ones are single. The crock's collar is accented by a repeating pattern of scalloped pickets. The underside of the collar is not glazed as is typical for crocks and bowls with defined collars. The bottom has a large molded star as a maker's mark.

⌒——Diamond Point Bowls——⌒

Two color examples of the Diamond Point pattern are shown. The diamond pattern is very clearly and deeply molded around the base of each of these examples with reverse pyramid accenting around the collar. The blue and white example is a very large bowl measuring 13½ inches across the top. It could certainly make a nice punchbowl for a country Christmas holiday gathering.

SIZES SHOWN: 7"h, 13½"w (large blue and
white bowl, previous page)
4¾"h, 7"w (medium blue and tan
bowl)
3"h, 6"w (small blue and tan bowl)
AVAILABILITY: Common pattern
COLORS: Blue and white; blue and tan
MINT VALUES: $75.00 – $125.00 each

The blue and tan coloration is shown above with the photo at right showing a close-up of the crown maker's mark on the bottom. The Diamond Point pattern was probably produced in a nesting set of five to seven bowls. While a complete nesting set was not available for photographing, if one were found, its value for the complete set could be estimated at $500.00.

Diamond Point Milk Crock with Bail

SIZE: 5¼"h, 10½"w
AVAILABILITY: Common pattern, rare in bail bowl form
COLORS: Blue and white, blue and tan
MINT VALUE: $200.00 – $250.00

The Diamond Point Milk Crock has the same pattern as the bowls presented above with the exception of its being in the bail bowl form with molded ears for attaching the wire bail. The collar is noticeably wider with more extended reverse pyramids.

◟◞— Diamonds with Reverse Picket Fence Crocks —◟◞

SIZES SHOWN:	3½"h, 9"w; Bottom, 6½"w (at top)
	3½"h, 11"w (at middle and bottom)
OTHER SIZES:	3"h, 9"w
	2½"h, 7"w
AVAILABILITY:	Common pattern
COLORS:	Blue and white
MINT VALUES:	$75.00 – $100.00 each

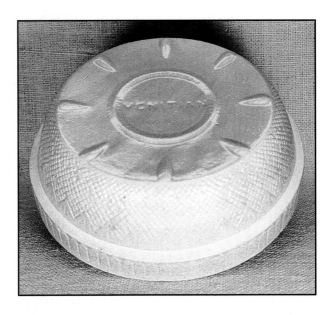

This example has a deeply cut diamond-like texture on its lower outside. It is rough to the touch which would be good when held by slippery hands. It is a low, wide bowl and was produced in a nesting set of at least three sizes. The pattern is slightly different from that of the Diamond Point bowls, indicating that several manufacturers may have produced similar wares. Notice the sunbursts just under the collar used as a transition between the diamond pattern and the reverse picket fence accenting around the collar. As noted in the right photo, the maker's mark "VENETIAN" is molded in the bottom which is totally glazed. The Venetian line was produced by the Roseville Pottery Company, Zanesville, Ohio. While these bowls were listed as baking dishes, the product line included custard cups, a bail bowl version, and lids for the baking dishes.

◟◞—— Fluted Scallops Bowl ——◟◞

This Fluted Scallops mixing bowl was probably used just as the name implies — for mixing biscuit dough, pie crusts, or another delectable concoction. This smaller bowl may also have been used as an everyday serving piece for vegetable dishes which would have been put directly on the dinner table. Since this is the only known size, nesting sets may not have been produced in this pattern.

SIZE: 5"h, 9"w
AVAILABILITY: Scarce pattern
COLORS: Green and cream
MINT VALUE: $75.00 – $100.00

~——Flying Birds Bowls——~

The Flying Birds pattern was used on a variety of pieces including several styles of bowls, pitchers, mugs, cookie jars, salt holders, butter crocks — in fact, an entire kitchen could have been equipped with the Flying Birds pattern which is quite desirable to most collectors.

A twig with flowers separates the flying birds which appear four times around the bowls, and clusters of flowers and stems are used to separate the birds around the collared bowl, which is an extremely rare example.

The body of the bowl is gracefully curved with a slightly fanned-out lip. The roping of flowers, which is traditional to the pattern, is used around the top and bottom of the bowls but not the collared bowl.

The Flying Birds pattern probably was produced in a nesting set of four to six bowls. While a complete nesting set was not available for photographing, if one were found, its value for the complete set could be estimated at $2,000.00.

SIZES: 4"h, 8¼"w (larger bowl, top row)
                 3½"h, 6½"w (smaller bowl, center row)
                 3½"h, 9"w (collared bowl, bottom row)
                 2"h, 4"w (berry bowl, previous page)
AVAILABILITY: Extremely rare pattern
COLORS: Blue and white
MINT VALUES: $250.00 – $300.00 each (larger and smaller bowls)
                 $150.00 – $200.00 (berry bowl)
                 $375.00 – $425.00 (collared bowl)

Grape Cluster Berry Bowl

SIZE: 1¾"h, 3w"
AVAILABILITY: Rare pattern
COLORS: Blue and white
MINT VALUE: $75.00 – $100.00

An unusually small piece marked "Majolica" on the bottom in very faint, incised lettering, this container may have been a berry bowl, a custard cup, or a salesman's sample. While it does have the same grape cluster pattern as a larger example in the Butter and Pastry Crocks section, it may have been part of a set. Each side has a grape cluster flanked by leaves with light blue coloration fading to almost white at the base. The top rim is accented with beading.

Greek Key Bowl

A wide center band of the Greek Key design boldly circles the bowl in white with very pale blue above and below the design. Small dotted lines frame the top and bottom of the design. A repeating pattern of Olympic pyramid steps accents the collar. Greek Key bowls were produced by the Red Wing Union Stoneware Company, Red Wing, Minnesota, in 6, 7, 8, 9, 10, 11, and 12 inch sizes. The DePasquales and Peterson indicate in *Red Wing Stoneware* (1983, Collector Books) that the 7, 9, and 11 inch sizes were added to the product line in the late 1920s, making the odd sizes less plentiful and even more rare than the even sizes which were introduced in the mid-teens. Greek Key bowls, especially the smaller sizes, were popular candidates for advertising messages, as was true for many Red Wing products.

SIZE: 5½"h, 11"w
AVAILABILITY: Rare pattern
COLORS: Blue and white
MINT VALUE: 6" – 10" sizes, $75.00 – $150.00
             11" – 12" sizes, $275.00 – $300.00
             With advertising, add 25%

Lovebirds Milk Crock with Bail

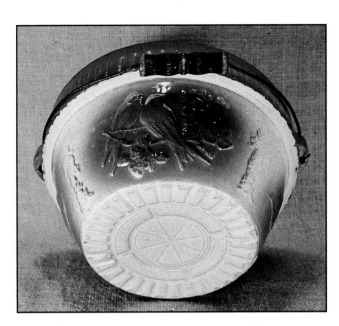

SIZE: 5½"h, 10½"w; Bottom, 6½"w
AVAILABILITY: Extremely rare pattern
COLORS: Blue and white
MINT VALUE: $350.00 – $400.00

The Lovebirds Milk Crock has the birds pattern on both sides of the bowl. They perch on a stem with a cluster of flowers to their right. The design is further accented by two small groupings of flowers on either side of the bird design highlighted in deep blue. This flower motif is the same as seen in the Lovebirds and Flying Birds patterns on other pieces, such as salt holders, butter crocks, and the cookie jar. The rich dark blue further enhances this piece and adds to its value. The bail is original. Notice the interesting mold pattern on the bottom which aids in heat circulation for stovetop uses.

Peacock Bowl and Custard Cup

SIZES: 3½"h, 6½"w (for bowl shown)
3"h, 3"w (custard cup)
AVAILABILITY: Extremely rare pattern
COLORS: Blue and white
MINT VALUES: Bowl, $450.00 – $500.00 each
Custard, $450.00 – $500.00

A custard cup and a small bowl in the elegant Peacock pattern are shown at left. The peacock, presented on both sides with palm trees in the background, is standing on a path of bricks. A top band of beading accents both the custard cup and bowl. These examples are considered to be truly rare. The Peacock pattern bowl may have been produced in other sizes; however, this is the only known size.

Reverse Pyramids and Reverse Picket Fences Bowl

SIZE: 5"h, 10"w
AVAILABILITY: Common pattern
COLORS: Blue and white and various solid shades
MINT VALUE: $65.00 – $95.00

Two color combinations of the Reverse Pyramids and Reverse Picket Fences bowl are shown above with excellent pattern detailing on each. Many examples are seen in various shades of solid blue while the white base with pale blue collar combination at right is somewhat unusual.

Reverse Pyramids and Reverse Picket Fences Milk Crock with Bail

SIZE: 5½"h, 11"w
AVAILABILITY: Common pattern
COLORS: Blue and white and various solid shades
MINT VALUE: $225.00 – $250.00

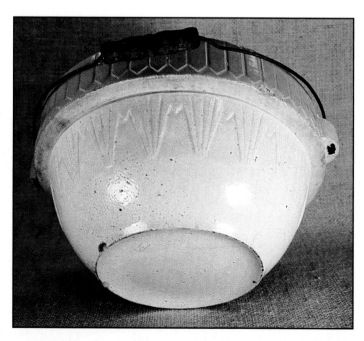

While bowls in this pattern are commonly seen, the milk crock is considered a rare find. The white base with blue collar is an unusual color combination. This example shows hard usage which would place it in the Good to Fair categories for pricing, thus reducing its value from that listed for mint condition. According to Kathryn McNerney's *Blue and White Stoneware* (1981, Collector Books), the Ruckels Stoneware Company in Monmouth, Illinois, originated the upside-down fence pattern on collars of bowls.

Ribbed Arches Bowl

SIZE: 5"h, 11"w
AVAILABILITY: Common pattern
COLORS: Blue and white, green and cream
MINT VALUE: Bowls, $65.00 – $95.00

Most commonly seen in green and cream colors ranging from pale to brilliant, the blue and white example shown is unusual, particularly with the richness of its color. The arches mold pattern around the collar is quite faint in these two examples. Because of its size, this bowl could have been quite handy for mixing a variety of everyday fare as well as special treats for a large family.

Scrolled Band Bowls

SIZES: 2½"h, 5"w
3"h, 6½"w
3½"h, 7½"w
4"h, 8½"w
4½"h, 9½"w
5½"h, 10½"w
6"h, 12½"w

AVAILABILITY: Common pattern
COLORS: Green and cream
MINT VALUES: $50.00 – $75.00 each
$400.00 – $500.00 for set of 7

Scrolled Band bowls appear to have been uniquely produced in green and cream with widely varying coloration from very pale diffused green to very crisp, rich green diffusing around the top and bottom. The scrolling around the collar provides a focal point which is enhanced by the detailed vertical pattern around the base of the bowl.

Produced in a range of sizes from very small to quite large, a complete set would consist of seven bowls. The Scrolled Band pattern provides a challenge to any molded stoneware collector to find a complete, color-matched collection. The pattern also appears to be unique for bowls as it has not been found on any other pieces.

Wedding Ring Bowls

SIZES: 2½"h, 5"w
3"h, 5½"w
3½"h, 6"w
3½"h, 7"w
3¾"h, 7¾"w
4"h, 8"w

AVAILABILITY: Scarce pattern

COLORS: Blue and white, green and cream

MINT VALUES: $500.00 – $800.00 for set of six
$100.00 – $150.00 for individuals

As one of the most desirable patterns of molded stoneware bowls, the Wedding Ring set was produced in a variety of sizes. Blue and white Wedding Ring bowls are the most commonly seen with green and cream ones being quite rare.

For both color combinations, variations from light to dark diffusing can be expected with color-matched sets being most preferred.

SIZE: 5¼"h, 11"w
AVAILABILITY: Rare size
COLORS: Blue and white, possibly in green and cream
MINT VALUE: $250.00 – $300.00

This large-sized bowl very distinctly shows the Wedding Ring pattern. A chain of connected rings with vertical lines encircles the body on a background of finely ribbed horizontal lines. The collar is detailed with sawtoothed scallops over vertical ribbing. A criss-cross band with centered dots accents the top and bottom of the base with the sawtoothed scallops over vertical ribbing completing the all-over pattern to the bottom. With so much fine pattern detailing, it is easy to understand why molds could become worn very quickly.

Electric Scientific Bail Bowl

SIZE: 5"h, 10"w
AVAILABILITY: Extremely rare
COLORS: Blue and white
MINT VALUE: $250.00 – $300.00

The Electric Scientific bowl was possibly a promotional item given with early electric stoves. The bottom carries the marking "Electric Scientific" and a fist holding lightning bolts. The bowl itself has a clear blue band and white base. The pattern on the body is a large diagonal lattice with small flowers in the gaps. A unique double layer of rickrack surrounds the collar. The bowl would be considered a rare find for any collector.

Blue Banded Bowls

SIZES: 5"h, 10"w (large bowl above)
3"h, 6½"w (small bowl on top at right)
4"h, 7¼"w (large bowl at right)
2¾"h, 5¼"w (small bowl at right)
AVAILABILITY: Common
COLORS: Blue and white
MINT VALUE: $55.00 – $75.00 each

Bowls were produced not only in a variety of patterns and styles but also in very simple forms such as the examples shown. Mold patterns and styles become secondary to the attention which the simple decoration of blue bands attracts.

Diffused Blue Nesting Bowls

SIZES: 5"h, 9¼"w (large bowl)
4½"h, 8¼"w (medium bowl)
3½"h, 6"w (small bowl)
AVAILABILITY: Scarce
COLORS: Blue and white
MINT VALUE: $45.00 – $65.00 each
$150.00 – $175.00 for set of 3

As a very plain yet appealing design of molded stoneware bowls, this set may have been some of the last wares made using the blue coloration which was widely applied on many types of pottery.

Spongeware Milk Crock with Bail

SIZE: 5"h, 10"w
AVAILABILITY: Rare form
COLORS: Blue and white
MINT VALUE: $300.00 – $350.00

Spongeware was often produced in styles and forms unlike other pieces of molded stoneware as is evidenced by this unique bail crock which rests on five small feet for heat and air circulation. Iron cooking pots which often had legs for elevation over hot fireplace coals may have inspired this crock's design. The original bail and worn feet indicate that this piece was well used.

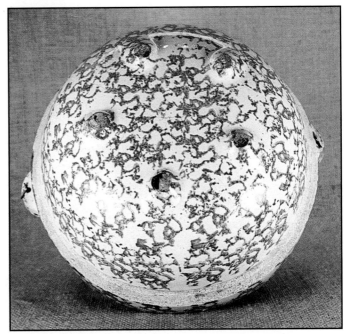

Spongeware Bowls

SIZE: 4½"h, 9"w
AVAILABILITY: Common
COLORS: Blue and white
MINT VALUE: $85.00 – $105.00

Nice dark blue sponging decorates this gracefully curved small bowl.

Spongeware Bowls, continued . . .

SIZES:	4"h, 9½"w (blue-banded bowl)
	4"h, 8"w (white-banded bowl)
AVAILABILITY:	Common
COLORS:	Blue and white
MINT VALUES:	$75.00 – $100.00 each

Sponging allowed makers to express their creativity by taking very plain pottery and dressing it up. These two examples using the same style of bowl were decorated to look quite different with one having a wide blue band to attract attention while the other uses two thin blue lines to create the illusion of one wide white band.

SIZES:	3"h, 9½"w (left)
	2¾"h, 8¼"w (right)
AVAILABILITY:	Scarce
COLORS:	Blue and white
MINT VALUES:	$75.00 – $125.00 each

A vegetable serving bowl is presented at left and a spongeware soup bowl is shown at right. Notice how the sponging is extended well over the rim inside the soup bowl.

SIZE: 5½"h, 10"w
AVAILABILITY: Common
COLORS: Blue and white
MINT VALUE: $175.00 – $225.00 each

Two examples of large spongeware mixing bowls with slightly different sponging decoration are shown above. The size of this bowl made it a perfect container for making biscuits and other doughs. Notice the arches as a part of the bowl pattern to which sponging was applied.

Miniature Bowls

Whether children's toys or salesman's samples, these miniature crocks are a favorite of many collectors. The small wire bails attach in the same manner as their larger counterparts. A stenciled windmill scene appears on both sides of the example shown at far left while the Reverse Pyramids and Reverse Picket Fences pattern is clear on the bowl at far left below.

SIZE: 2"h, 4"w (for all)
AVAILABILITY: Scarce
COLORS: Blue and white
MINT VALUE: $125.00 – $150.00 each

Section VIII – Utilitarian Kitchenwares

With so much time spent in food preparation, the kitchen of yesteryear was not only the hub of cooking activity but also a favorite gathering spot in the household for family, neighbors, and friends. Kitchens furnished with a large round oak dining table as well as work tables, cabinets, and wood-fired cooking and heating stoves provided a cozy atmosphere.

The kitchen of long ago suffered no deprivation in the area of gadgetry as any search of the subject in reference guides will verify. With respect to molded stoneware, the same is certainly true. In addition to the multitude of bowls, pitchers, mugs, rolling pins, coffee and tea pots, butter and pastry crocks, and salt holders which have already received attention, a variety of utilitarian kitchenwares was produced to facilitate productivity and pleasure in the preparation of food.

From grease jars to whipped cream jars, batter pails to bean crocks, and meat tenderizers to roasters, the gamut of molded stoneware gadgetry and containers produced to equip a kitchen is almost an area of specialization within itself. Even though examples are not shown in this section, several styles and shapes of large baking and roasting crocks were produced. Because of their size and probable hard usage, few have survived.

With so much intense wear, many of the utilitarian kitchen pieces did not go unscathed from chips and, even more tragic, total breakage. Thus, do not be dismayed upon acquiring one of these items in a less than pristine state. Rather, consider the imperfections as marks of character developed in the warm, loving environment of mother's kitchen.

Batter Pails

Stenciled Flowers

SIZE: 5"h, 8"w
AVAILABILITY: Scarce pattern
COLORS: Blue and white
MINT VALUE: $200.00 – $225.00

A vine with large stenciled flowers and leaves circles the entire exterior sides of this batter pail. A wire bail to facilitate pouring would have originally been attached.

Basketweave and Morning Glory

Stenciled Wildflower

SIZE: 5"h, 7"w
AVAILABILITY: Scarce pattern
COLORS: Blue and white
MINT VALUE: $275.00 – $300.00

SIZE: 5"h, 8"w
AVAILABILITY: Scarce pattern
COLORS: Blue and white
MINT VALUE: $250.00 – $275.00

The top rim of the Stenciled Wildflower batter pail (above left) is capped with a blue band while the sides are decorated with the wildflower design which is repeated four times around the pail. The pulled lip pouring spout on batter pails is small. The popular Basketweave and Morning Glory pattern on a batter pail (above right) is a rare find. A prong at each end of uthe wire bail on batter pails inserts into a small hole made slightly into the pottery but not piercing the interior.

Boston Baked Beans Crock

"Boston Baked Beans" in large scrolling letters graces one side of this crock while a cluster of flowing leaves embellishes the opposite. The lid which sits securely inside a rim may have a round knob or an acorn-style finial. Although these crocks are frequently seen, they still command high prices. The blue on these crocks may be in a swirl or a diffused application.

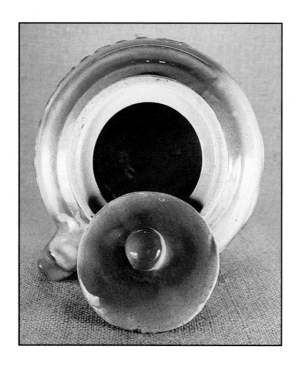

SIZE: 7"h (without lid), 7"w; lid, 4½"d
AVAILABILITY: Common
COLORS: Blue and white
MINT VALUE: $450.00 – $500.00

Cottage Cheese Press

SIZE: 9"h (when stacked), 7"w; press, 4½"d
Large bottom: 5½"h, 7"w
Top section: 4½"h, 6½"w
AVAILABILITY: Extremely rare
COLORS: Blue and white
MINT VALUE: $1,200.00 – $1,500.00

A cottage cheese press is among the most rare pieces for any collection. The top section has a strainer bottom. The press (or what appears to be a lid) has a small handle and is used to squeeze excess liquid from freshly made batches of cottage cheese. The seaweed style decoration and banding on this piece's exterior are in a vibrant blue.

Creamer with Side Spout

SIZE: 5"h, 3"w
AVAILABILITY: Rare
COLORS: Blue and white
MINT VALUE: $200.00 – $225.00

This very unusually styled pitcher is a creamer with the pulled spout placed on the side to make pouring cream into a cup of coffee more convenient. The simple pattern has raised bands circling the body with light blue diffusing around the top and bottom.

Egg Bucket

SIZE: 5½"h, 6"w
AVAILABILITY: Scarce
COLORS: White with blue bands
MINT VALUE: $235.00 – $275.00

    An egg bucket would have been used to gather and/or store eggs fresh from the hen house. Vertical lines run from the top to the bottom, giving a barrel-type look. Blue and white bands encircle the body. The wooden handle on a wire bail attaches to pulled ears just under the top rim.

Meat Tenderizer (Stenciled Wildflower)

    This is an unusual form to find in pottery. The stenciled wildflower design appears on both sides between top and bottom blue bands. The bottom plate is roughly textured. Notice that a screw holds the pottery to the long, wooden handle.

    The Wildflower stenciling was used widely on a variety of molded stoneware. Coordinated kitchens are certainly not an invention of modern designers since, as shown below, a variety of pieces could be acquired in the same style.

SIZE: 3"h, 12"l (with handle)
AVAILABILITY: Extremely rare
COLORS: Blue and white
MINT VALUE: $500.00 – $650.00

Spear Point and Flower Panels Measuring Cup

SIZE: 5¼"h, 5½"w (across top)
AVAILABILITY: Rare
COLORS: Blue and white, also in yellow ware
MINT VALUE: $325.00 – $400.00

Whether measuring flour or milk, mixing cornbread, beating eggs, or stirring up a pie, the measuring cup was an invaluable vessel for any kitchen. Measuring cups typically received fairly hard usage, accounting for the condition in which many examples are presently found. Notice that the applied handle is squared.

Spongeware Mush Cup and Saucer

SIZE: 4"h, 5"w (overall)
AVAILABILITY: Scarce
COLORS: Blue and white
MINT VALUE: $175.00 – $225.00

This cup was used for serving hot grain cereals such as mush, a cooked cornmeal mixture similar to grits. The circle handle is quite unusual particularly with the support bar under it. The close sponging on this piece creates an almost streaked effect.

Spongeware Plate (Ulysses S. Grant Impression)

SIZE: 12"d
AVAILABILITY: Rare
COLORS: Blue and white
MINT VALUE: $250.00 – $300.00

    This decorative spongeware plate features a bust of Ulysses S. Grant in the center. The outer edge of the plate has a raised ivy leaf design.

Refrigerator Jar

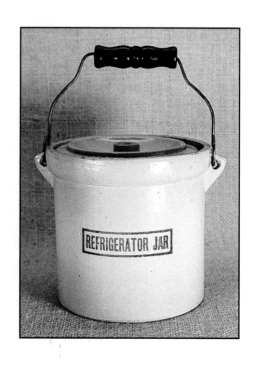

SIZE: 6"h, 6"w
AVAILABILITY: Scarce
COLORS: Blue and white
MINT VALUE: $250.00 – $300.00

    This refrigerator jar is probably a later production, after the invention and the mass production of refrigerators in the 1920s. The design is simple with a lid that sits inside a deep rim and a handle attached to ears built into the mold.

Syrup Pitcher

SIZE: 5½"h, 4"w
AVAILABILITY: Rare
COLORS: Blue and white
MINT VALUE: $350.00 – $400.00

This syrup pitcher has open white areas on the body and is sparsely sponged in a dark blue pawprint pattern. The lid with a small knob sits in a lipped rim inside the top of the pitcher.

Vinegar Cruet

SIZE: 4¼"h, 3"w
AVAILABILITY: Extremely rare
COLORS: Blue and white
MINT VALUE: $275.00 – $325.00

This vinegar cruet is quite small, standing approximately four inches tall. Whether or not it originally had a pottery stopper is unknown. Very simple in design with a delicate applied handle, it is highlighted with diffused blue around the top and the base.

Whipped Cream Jars

LARGE SIZE: 7"h, 9½"w (next page)
SMALL SIZE: 4¾"h, 6¾"w (right)
AVAILABILITY: Extremely rare
COLORS: Blue and white
MINT VALUES: $475.00 – $550.00 each

Whipped cream jars are quite unusual kitchenwares intended for a specific use. Cream could be skimmed off the milk, placed in this jar, and whipped in the same container. The design is very plain with bands of diffused blue around the top and bottom of the container as well as around the rim of the lid. The lid had a large mushroom-style knob and sits in a deeply recessed lip around the top of the jar. The top band of the jar has two grip handles which extend on each side.

Daisy and Waffle Grease Jar

SIZE: 4"h, 4½"w
AVAILABILITY: Extremely rare
COLORS: Blue and white
MINT VALUE: $225.00 – $250.00

The Daisy and Waffle pattern is rare in the form of a grease jar. Its size is quite small; note that the holes for the wire bail were never cut. The recessed button lid fits securely over a raised, unglazed rim protruding from the body.

Dragonfly and Flower Grease Jar

SIZE: 4"h, 5"w
AVAILABILITY: Rare
COLORS: Solid light blue
MINT VALUE: $325.00 – $375.00

The is the smallest of a six-size series of the Dragonfly and Flower covered crocks intended for multiple uses including grease, butter, lard, pastries, and food storage. This series was produced by the Logan Pottery Company of Logan, Ohio. Both sides of the body are the same with a flower framed by a medallion of leaves and flanked on each side by a dragonfly.

Flying Birds Grease Jar

SIZE: 4"h, 4½"w
AVAILABILITY: Extremely rare
COLORS: Blue and white
MINT VALUE: $450.00 – $500.00

The flying bird motif appears on both sides of this rare grease jar in the quite desirable Flying Birds pattern. The top and bottom are accented by a row of flowers. The dark blue coloration on this example makes it even more attractive.

Wesson Oil Jar

SIZE: 5½"h, 4½"w
AVAILABILITY: Common
COLORS: Blue and white
MINT VALUE: $90.00 – $110.00

This piece was used as a grease jar and was probably given away as a promotional item early in the product's beginning. The bottom of the jar is rounded which probably facilitated the making of mayonnaise.

Red Wing Beater Jar

SIZE: 5"h, 5"w
AVAILABILITY: Common
COLORS: Blue and white
MINT VALUE: $75.00 – $100.00

This beater jar would have been used to beat eggs, cream, and salad dressings. The opposite side shows the advertising message which indicates that this was probably a promotional item for the store.

~~~~Brickers Cookie Jar~~~~

    Diffused blue top coloration fading to an all-white bottom accents this Brickers cookie jar. "Brickers" is a Pennsylvania name for a kind of cookie popular in that state. The writing appears on one side only. The lid is simple, all blue, and sits inside a deeply recessed top rim.

SIZE: 7½"h, 7½"w; lid, 5¼"d
AVAILABILITY: Extremely rare
COLORS: Blue and white
MINT VALUE: $500.00 – $600.00

Flying Birds Cookie Jar

This cookie jar has the lovebirds on one side and the flying birds on the reverse. Flower clusters adorn the sides as transitions between the lovebirds and flying birds motifs. As is characteristic of the pattern, the top and bottom as well as the rim of the lid are accented by a band of small flowers. The rounded knob on the domed lid is large enough for an easy grip; yet, numerous children probably got into trouble for breaking the lid of their mother's prized cookie jar. The flying birds motif is repeated four times around the lid.

SIZE: 9"h (with lid), 6¾"w
AVAILABILITY: Extremely rare
COLORS: Blue and white
MINT VALUE: $1,000.00 – $1,200.00

Swan Toothpick Holders

SIZE: 2"h, 3½"l
AVAILABILITY: Scarce, not commonly seen
COLORS: Blue, green, and red
MINT VALUES: $75.00 – $100.00 each

The graceful swan is the same on both sides. The head has a delicate opening as it bends to the body. The feathers are clearly shown with variances in the glaze color. Note that the eyes are painted on top of the glaze in some of the examples. The variety of colors makes for an interesting grouping.

Reproduction Novelty Toothpick Holders

SIZE: 2"h, 1"w
AVAILABILITY: Scarce
COLORS: Blue and white
MINT VALUES: $20.00 – $30.00 each

These toothpick holders appeared during the 1980s when the country look became so popular. They are new and were apparently never produced in older versions. They are miniatures of some of the most desirable pitchers. From left to right: Eagle, Indian in War Bonnet, Grazing Cows, Lincoln Head.

Pie Plates

SIZES FOR ALL: 1½"h, 9"w
AVAILABILITY: Scarce
COLORS: Blue and white
MINT VALUES: $150.00 – $200.00 each

The lattice pie plate above has little space for design but manages to have a surround of latticework with the word "PATENTED" in the mold along with a large star said to be the mark of the Star Stoneware Company of Akron, Ohio. The plain-sided pie plate at right has raised bands on the bottom to help circulate the heat and brown a bottom crust. The maker's mark "IXL" is in the center of the bottom.

—Apple Blossom Water Cooler—

The Apple Blossom pattern was among the most intricate and beautiful produced in any piece and is especially outstanding on the water cooler. In large, Old English letters highlighted in dark blue, "Ice Water" clearly denotes the intended use of this piece. Graceful stems of apple blossoms frame the front side of the cooler which has a diagonal lattice background all over. A nickel-plated spigot is installed at the bottom front.

While pictured only in Apple Blossom and Polar Bear examples, water coolers were produced in other desirable patterns including the Elk and Cupid as well as a variety of banded styles, many of which were advertising pieces. The green "Deer in the Woods" sand jar in the Household Section later was most likely a cooler also. The only difference between a sand jar and a cooler was that the hole for the spigot was not cut out.

SIZE: 17"h, 15"w
AVAILABILITY: Extremely rare
COLORS: Blue and white
MINT VALUE: $2,000.00 – $2,500.00

A chain pattern encircles the top and bottom of this Apple Blossom water cooler while a large dark blue "4" in a laurel twig medallion on the back side indicates the cooler's capacity to be four gallons. Apple blossoms surround the center knob on the lid with an unglazed band toward the outer edge.

Polar Bear Water Cooler

SIZE: 23½"h, 14"w
AVAILABILITY: Extremely rare
COLORS: Blue and white
MINT VALUE: $2,000.00 – $2,500.00

The Polar Bear cooler is a huge piece standing nearly two feet tall. Both sides are identical with the majestic polar bear standing on an ice cap in a beaded medallion on a waffle background. "Ice Water" subtly indicates the vessel's intended use. The spigot is missing on the example shown. The lid is embossed with intricate bands of waffle and raised dots centered with a gracefully designed knob.

——Basketweave and Morning Glory Canisters——

CANISTERS:
          SIZE: 6¾"h, 5¼"w (at widest point)
AVAILABILITY: Generally scarce
       COLORS: Blue and white
MINT VALUES: Complete set: $4,000.00 – $5,000.00

Tea, $350.00	Cookie Jar, $750.00
Beans, $450.00	("Put Your Fist In")
Salt, $350.00	Tobacco, $750.00
Raisins, $350.00	Large Crackers, $550.00
Sugar, $350.00	Small Crackers, $450.00
Coffee, $350.00	

The Basketweave and Morning Glory canister pattern has a scroll over the basketweave pattern that is stenciled with the contents to be put inside. The reverse side of these canisters (bottom photo) has the morning glory decoration. The lid barely fits on the top of the canister which helps to explain why so many were broken. The top photo shows the size difference between the canister and spice containers.

SPICE JARS:
          SIZE: 4¼"h, 3"w (at widest point)
AVAILABILITY: Scarce
       COLORS: Blue and white
MINT VALUES: Each: $150.00 – $200.00
                      Complete set: $1,500.00 – $2,000.00

Basketweave and Morning Glory Canisters, continued . . .

At left, the raisins, sugar, and coffee Basketweave and Morning Glory canisters; below, tea, beans, and salt canisters. Notice the slightly different coloration and width of the blue diffusing around the top and bottom. Because the beans canister is quite difficult to find, it commands a higher price in the market place.

The small basketweave spice jars mirror the large canisters except for the absence of the morning glory on the back side. The scroll and spice name only appears on one side. The lids barely sit on the top of each spice jar. Shown here are the six basic spice jars: ginger, allspice, cinnamon, cloves, nutmeg, and pepper.

Above are examples of the more expensive cookie and tobacco canisters. Shown at right are the reverse sides of these same pieces. The original cookie jar lid (above left) has been replaced with a more expensive, although not original, tobacco jar lid. The cavity in the high domed lid of the tobacco canister is said to have been used to hold a fresh slice of apple for keeping the tobacco moist and for flavoring. Shown below are top and inside angles of the tobacco jar lid.

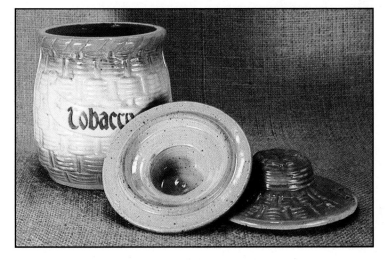

Basketweave and Morning Glory Canisters, continued . . .

The large and the small Basketweave and Morning Glory crackers canisters are shown above to note the size difference. A lid with excellent mold pattern is shown below. Notice the flower in the center of the knob. These lids have very shallow rims which, when combined with their very flat knobs, provided reason for much breakage.

Three lids for Basketweave and Morning Glory canisters are shown above. Two are originals, and the third was made by a potter who specializes in repairs and missing parts for molded stoneware. Can you tell which is the newly made lid?

The owner has clearly marked the underside of the newly made lid. It is the one on the right in both photos. Good job, right?

∽————Various Canister and Spice Jar Styles————∽

Left to right:
  Basketweave and Morning Glory (Sugar)
  Ovoid Stenciled Wildflower (Farina)
  Straight-sided Stenciled Small Snowflake (Coffee)
  Straight-sided Stenciled Large Snowflake (Salt)
    (Lid matches Snowflake pattern)

Various styles of canisters were produced as can be seen above. A full set is rarely found available for sale; therefore, one could spend his or her entire life collecting the six canisters or six spice jars which typically constitute a set.

Various Canisters and Spice Jar Styles, continued . . .

Straight-sided Diffused Blue with gold stenciling (Salt, Cinnamon)

Ovoid Stenciled Wildflower (Raisins)

CANISTERS:

SIZE: 6½"h, 5"w
(approximate dimensions for all styles except Greek Key)
AVAILABILITY: Scarce
COLORS: Blue and white
MINT VALUES: Each: $225.00 – $275.00
Complete set: $1,750.00 – $2,500.00

SPICE JARS:

SIZE: 4¼"h, 3"w
AVAILABILITY: Scarce
COLORS: Blue and white
MINT VALUES: Each: $100.00 – $150.00
Complete set: $700.00 – $900.00

Grape Cluster spice jar and Greek Key canister are shown at left. Both are missing original lids which greatly reduces their value.

Section IX – Household

While the vast majority of molded stoneware production was aimed at kitchenwares, the rest of the house provided opportunities for manufacturers as well. Modern day ceramic sinks, tubs, and toilets can trace their own heritage to earlier pottery pieces in the forms of washbowl and pitcher sets, chamber pots, and other utilitarian household forms which were produced to facilitate sanitation.

Today we all take running water for granted, not to mention having hot, running water at the turn of a knob. Imagine all the water you now use having to be drawn from a well with a bucket and pulley, or being carried in from a nearby stream, or having to be collected from rain water run-off. If you wanted it hot, it had to be warmed in the sun, set near the fire, or placed on the stove. Some woodstoves had the luxury of a water reservoir that constantly held warm water as long as the stove was fired, but it, too, had to be kept full.

Taking a bath often proved to be an extended ordeal. Those who had a tub of some kind did well to use it periodically. When they did, an entire family would use the same water. The grownups went first and were followed by all of the children. During the week, "washing up" meant using a washbowl and pitcher. Cold fresh water was kept in the pitcher and poured into the bowl as needed. A smaller pitcher of hot water was used to achieve the correct temperature in the bowl.

Washbowl and pitcher sets were produced in all shapes and sizes. They also range from the very fancy to the simplest of forms. All are highly collectible since a number of patterns were produced. Many have accessory pieces to match such as chamber pots, toothbrush holders, smaller matching hot water pitchers, and soap dishes such as seen with the Fishscale and Wild Roses grouping. Putting together a set in the same color tones can be quite a challenge as you may find a piece here and there in your pursuits. Bowls in perfect shape are not common. Due to the regular use they received, cracks and chips are common.

Washbowl and pitcher sets tend to evoke and complete the homey look of bygone days like none other when displayed on an old washstand for which they were intended.

Soap dishes were produced in their own unique patterns as well as in the patterns used for washbowl and pitcher sets. The full washstand sets often included the washbowl and pitcher, a hot water pitcher, a toothbrush holder, often a powder dish, and yes, usually a soap dish. Soap dishes are just as practical and usable today as they were when originally produced and are certainly a nice complement for any modern bathroom. They were designed to have an embossed pattern in a flat dish that allowed the moisture from the soap to drain.

Soap dishes have been heavily reproduced; therefore, collectors should BE CAREFUL. Some reproductions are quite good, and it is often difficult to distinguish from those which were originally produced.

The mere thought of using a chamber pot and having it sit beside the bed you are sleeping in is, well, not a pleasant thought. The alternative, however, is even more unpleasant. Think of what an ordeal it would be to go to an outhouse several yards from the comfort of your bed during a cold night or even worse, in rain or snow. Even a summertime trip might be an event should you encounter a snake or other creature. A chamber pot is a nostalgic reminder of a time we are all glad is past for most of us today.

One of the funniest stories involving molded stoneware was heard several years ago at a market booth that contained a fine stoneware chamber pot and lid which were attracting great attention. A nice couple walked up and commented that they had one just like it and it was just great in the winter. Everyone around looked at the woman strangely when she said it would keep soup nice and hot on the table. Needless to say, she was quite shocked when she learned what her serving piece was. It can only be hoped that her guests did not know the pot's true use. Wonder if she is still using it? This story fully exhibits the need to be informed about what you are buying and using.

A chamber pot looks great beside a bed or in a bath. The open top types look good holding small towels and soaps. Due to their frequent use, the ones with lids are often chipped at the rim. The lids are often broken or missing entirely, but occasionally one may see spare lids for sale which can be matched with a pot which has no lid. A nice lid can also be hung on the wall with a plate hanger. Chamber pots often match dresser sets consisting of a bowl and pitcher, toothbrush holder, and hot water pitcher.

Footwarmers were quite a clever invention — portable heaters. Today they would come in handy at an outside winter auction or football game. During their era of greatest use, people tried most anything to beat the winter cold as warmth typically came from a wood stove or fireplace that, at best, very unevenly warmed a room. Traveling by wagon or in an early car also meant producing your own warmth during the travel time. Very early footwarmers held live coals in a tray. The pottery types held hot water. Stories are told that they were often taken to bed and placed near the foot of the bed to warm cold feet. They were taken to church, on long trips, and were an especially nice accoutrement for a sleigh ride in the snow. They often contained pieces of wax that helped to hold the heat. If you hear something "rattling" inside one, do not be alarmed since it is more than likely the remaining broken wax.

There is also a small-size footwarmer that is referred to as both a salesman's sample and handwarmer. We will let you decide which you want to call it.

Cuspidors were once as common in the household as any other everyday item. It was an acceptable practice for both the men and women of the household to use some form of a tobacco product. The men traditionally chewed tobacco; the women used snuff. Snuff products were "poured" into the lower lip or dipped with a small stick fashioned into a brushlike form by fraying the end. A chew of tobacco was held in the lower lip or jaw. Since the tobacco mixed with saliva, cuspidors were maintained for spitting since no one wanted to swallow the strong tobacco juice. Cuspidors were filled with shavings or sand and changed regularly since it was such an unsanitary practice.

Cuspidors were produced in a variety of patterns and are a nice addition to a varied collection. They are easily displayed and can even be used to hold flowers.

Apple Blossom Washbowl and Pitcher

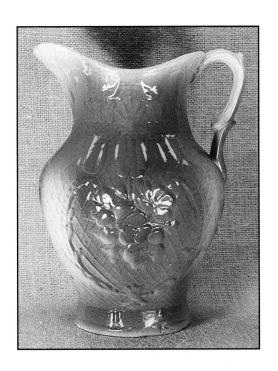

SIZES: Washbowl: 4"h, 15"w
Pitcher: 11½"h, 8"w (at widest point)
AVAILABILITY: Extremely rare pattern
COLORS: Blue and white
MINT VALUE: $450.00 – $600.00+

The pitcher bears a stately cluster of apple blossoms highlighted in a medallion on a diamond-shaped background. Intricate molding details are common in all pieces using the Apple Blossom pattern.

Basketweave and Morning Glory Washstand Set

SIZES: Washbowl: 4"h, 15"w
Pitcher: 10"h, 6"w (at widest point)
Hot water pitcher: 7½"h, 5"w (at widest point)
Toothbrush holder: 5"h, 3"w (at widest point)
Soap dish: 3¼"h, 5"w
AVAILABILITY: Rare
COLORS: Blue and white
MINT VALUES: Complete set: $1,750.00 – $2,000.00
Washbowl and pitcher: $650.00 – $750.00
Hot water pitcher: $200.00 – $250.00
Toothbrush holder: $150.00 – $175.00
Soap dish: $175.00 – $225.00

An elegant bowl and pitcher set is found in this stately pattern with spurred handle. The basketweave pattern circles the perimeter of the bowl. The soap dish, water pitcher and toothbrush holder pictured below add the final complement to this entire set. Notice the unusually shaped toothbrush holder and, as shown below, the insert in the soap dish to facilitate drainage. The star on the lid may denote a manufacturer's trademark. A covered chamber pot in the Basketweave and Morning Glory pattern is shown later in this section.

Beaded Rose Cluster and Spear Points Pitcher

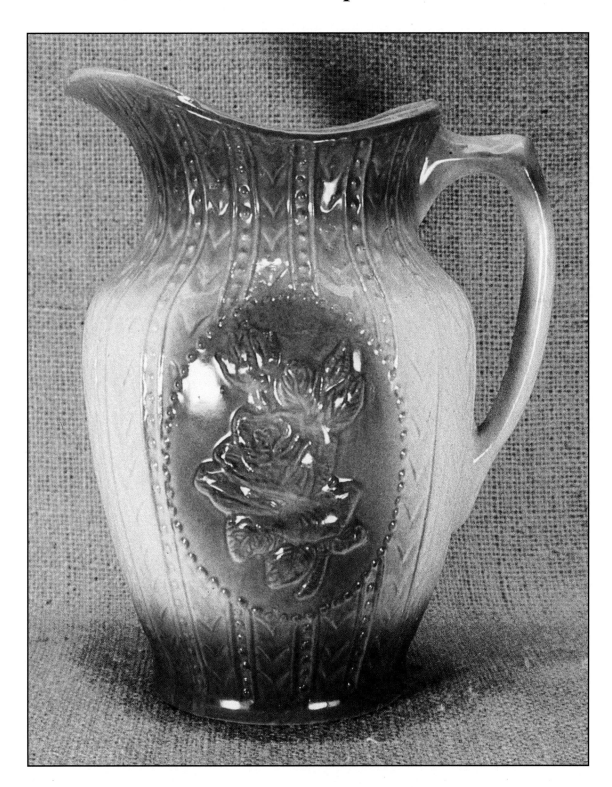

SIZE: Pitcher: 12"h, 8½"w (at widest point)
AVAILABILITY: Extremely rare pattern
COLORS: Blue and white
MINT VALUE: $650.00 – $700.00

The eye focuses on an open rose cluster in a medallion surrounded by a row of beads. The body of this large pitcher is covered with panels of spear points and vertical columns of beading. This larger table pitcher was part of a washbowl and pitcher set. Smaller versions can also be found in this pattern and are referred to as hot water pitchers which were also part of a washstand set. A complete washstand set in this pattern would certainly be one degree beyond extremely rare.

Bowknot with Roses Transfer Decal Washstand Set

SIZE: Washbowl: 4"h, 15"w
Pitcher: 11"h, 8½"w (at widest point)
Toothbrush holder: 5½"h, 4"w (at widest point)
Soap dish: 2½"h, 5½"w
Shaving mug: 2½"h, 5½"w
Chamber pot: 13"h, 8½"w
AVAILABILITY: Common pattern, rare with transfer decals
COLORS: Blue and white with roses transfer
MINT VALUES: Complete set: $1,750.00 – $2000.00
Washbowl and pitcher: $450.00 – $550.00
Toothbrush holder: $150.00 – $175.00
Soap dish: $225.00 – $275.00
Shaving mug: $150.00 – $175.00
Chamber pot:(next page): $375.00 – $400.00

This grouping shows a soap dish with lid, toothbrush holder, and shaving mug. The Bowknot pattern with roses transfer decal is found on each piece. Note the insert in the soap dish to facilitate drainage. The washbowl also bears the roses transfer decal. The Bowknot pattern is also seen in plain versions without the transfer decals. Values for plain versions would be approximately 25 percent lower.

The underlying pattern is the bowknot as seen near the top rim and on the lid. This piece is enhanced by the colorful rose transfer decals on each side and on the lid. The lid has also been detailed with gold lines around the rim and on the handle.

∽————Bowknot with Stenciling Washbowl and Pitchers————∽

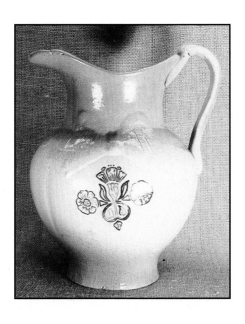

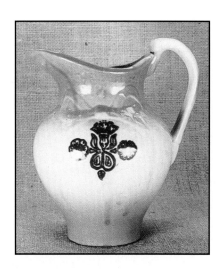

SIZES: Pitcher: 10½"h, 7½"w (at widest point)
Hot water pitcher: 7½"h, 5½"w (at widest point)
AVAILABILITY: Scarce pattern
COLORS: Blue and white
MINT VALUES: Pitchers: $175.00 – $225.00 each
Bowl and pitcher set: $450.00 – $500.00

These beautiful pitchers were parts of a washstand set with the large one (left) being a partner in a bowl and pitcher set and the smaller one (center and right) being used for hot water. The stencil is only on one side. Note the tied bow in the pattern at the top of each piece on both sides. Covered chamber pots, toothbrush holders, and covered soap dishes were also produced in this pattern.

Daisies Washbowl and Pitcher

SIZES: Pitcher: 10"h, 7¼"w (at widest point)
            Bowl: 3½"h, 13"w
AVAILABILITY: Rare pattern
COLORS: Blue and white
MINT VALUE: Bowl and pitcher set: $375.00 – $400.00

This deep blue bowl and pitcher set is accented by a small cluster of daisies and leaves in the center of the pitcher on each side. The bottom of the bowl, as seen at right, has bubbled glazing which is often referred to as "rice marks." Such markings on a piece may denote a snafu in the glazing and firing process.

Fishscale and Wild Roses Washstand Set

The smaller bowl and pitcher set on the left typifies an example of the deep blue hues common in stoneware. This smaller size is often referred to as a child's set. Note the light and dark patterning around the bowl. At right, a larger version of the pattern is shown. The center cluster of wild roses as well as the rows of fishscales has clear, distinct pattern. Note that the bowl has a blue-banded rim and white exterior.

The green color is rare in this smaller-size bowl and pitcher. Note the color variation between the bowl and the pitcher. The possibility exists that this duo was "married" (pieces from different sets) or that they were fired at different times, resulting in the varied green hues.

The bottom of this green bowl is an example of swirling for decorative purposes. The photos on the following page show the blue and white pitcher and the matching bowl, which is also swirled, separately.

SIZES: Large washbowl: 4"h, 15½"w
Large pitcher: 11"h, 6½"w
Small washbowl: 3½"h, 13"w
Small pitcher: 9"h, 6¼"w
Hot water pitcher: 6½"h, 4½"w
Toothbrush holder: 4¾"h, 3½"w
Powder box: 2½"h, 5½"w
Soap dish: 1"h, 4½"w
Chamber pot: 5½"h, 9½"w
Covered chamber pot: 9½"h (with lid), 8"w

AVAILABILITY: Common pattern
COLORS: Blue and white, green and cream
MINT VALUES: Complete set: $1,750.00 – $2,000.00
Large washbowl and pitcher: $450.00 – $550.00
Small washbowl and pitcher: $450.00 – $550.00
Hot water pitcher: $150.00 – $175.00
Toothbrush holder: $150.00 – $175.00
Powder box: $225.00 – $275.00
Soap dish: $150.00 – $200.00
Chamber pot: $250.00 – $325.00
Covered chamber pot: $375.00 – $400.00

Fishscale and Wild Roses Washstand Set, continued . . .

The cluster above shows the blue soap dish, powder jar, hot water pitcher, and toothbrush holder.

Notice the distinct fishscale pattern in the powder box lid.

This grouping consists of the green soap dish (pattern not distinct, but rare in green), the washbowl and pitcher, and the hot water pitcher.

Fishscale and Wild Roses Chamber Pot

An example is presented above of a green chamber pot (alias "thundermug") with vibrant color and deep, clear pattern. The blue covered chamber pot below has the wild roses cluster on each side in a beaded medallion. The body is covered in the fishscale pattern, and the lid handle is flanked on either side by the rose cluster in a medallion.

Rose Transfer Pitchers

SIZES: Pitchers at left: 7½"h, 5"w
Below left: 7½"h, 5½"w
Below right: 6½"h, 5"w
AVAILABILITY: Rare, not commonly seen
COLORS: Blue and white with roses transfer
MINT VALUE: $175.00 – $225.00 each

The brilliant roses transfer on the pitcher at left with fluted spout is stunning. Most likely, each of these pitchers was part of a washstand set and they were probably used as hot water pieces.

These rose transfer pitchers have different patterns. The left example is a bowtie pattern while the one on the right has simple vertical lines with ribboning just above the decal.

Sponge with Blue Bands Washstand Set

SIZES: Washbowl: 5"h, 14"w
Pitcher: 10"h, 7½"w (at widest point)
Hot water pitcher: 7"h, 5½"w (at widest point)
Soap dish: 5"l, 3½"w
Chamber pot: 5"h, 8½"w
AVAILABILITY: Rare pattern
COLORS: Blue and white
MINT VALUES: Complete set: $1,500.00 – $1,750.00
Wash bowl and pitcher: $650.00 – $750.00
Hot water pitcher: $225.00 – $300.00
Soap dish: $125.00 – $150.00
Chamber pot: $225.00 – $250.00

Assembling a complete washstand set in any pattern can certainly be a challenge since it is rare to find all pieces available for purchase at one time. Assembling a complete washstand set in spongeware can provide an even greater challenge since it is typically more scarce. Presented above are the soap dish, washbowl and pitcher, and hot water pitcher in this urn-shaped form. The blue bands are seen on both the pitchers and bowl but do not appear on the soap dish. The gentle curve in the applied handles on each pitcher adds an element of grace.

The grouping below highlights the "earthworm" sponging effect at the top and bottom of the chamber pot. Notice the differences in the handles.

Presented at right is a view of the inside of a bowl with sponging around the rim and in the bottom. Examples of two blue-banded pitchers below show the varied styles and shapes available. Notice the gracefully flared pouring spout on the piece below right.

This banded hot water pitcher at left with crisp, clear, and vibrant sponging tapers into a bulbous bottom with a slightly pinched pouring spout.

SIZE: Pitcher: 7"h, 5½"w (at widest point)
AVAILABILITY: Rare pattern
COLORS: Blue and white
MINT VALUE: $275.00 – $325.00

SIZES: Pitcher: 8"h, 6"w (at widest point)
Bowl: 4"h, 12"w
AVAILABILITY: Rare pattern
COLORS: Blue, green and white
MINT VALUE: Bowl and pitcher set: $375.00 – $400.00

The small blue and green sponged washbowl and pitcher with a bold blue band shown above reflect a change from the more commonly seen blue sponged pieces.

SIZES: Washbowl: 5"h, 14"w
Pitcher: 10"h, 7½"w (at widest point)
AVAILABILITY: Rare pattern
COLORS: Blue and white
MINT VALUE: $650.00 – $750.00

Spongeware was produced in a variety of shapes and sizes. This washbowl and pitcher set is quite similar to those previously shown. With very crisp, clear sponging, flared lip, and the "cattail" style applied handle, it is an excellent example.

This large spongeware pitcher at left has an unusual shape and very close sponging. It was probably part of a washbowl and pitcher set.

SIZE: 10"h, 7"w (at widest point)
AVAILABILITY: Common
COLORS: Blue and white
MINT VALUE: $275.00 – $325.00

Earthworm Sponge Washbowl and Pitcher

SIZES: Pitcher: 10"h, 8½"w (at widest point)
Bowl: 5½"h, 15"w
AVAILABILITY: Extremely rare pattern
COLORS: Blue and white
MINT VALUE: $1,200.00 – $1,500.00

This beautiful set is sponged in the earthworm design. A white area is left on each piece to accentuate the sponging. The pitcher spout is elegantly flared.

Wildflower Hot Water Pitcher

SIZE: 8"h, 6"w (at widest point)
AVAILABILITY: Rare pattern, not commonly seen
COLORS: Blue and white
MINT VALUE: $175.00 – $225.00
(Complete set with washbowl and pitcher, toothbrush holder, soap dish, and hot water pitcher: $1,200.00 – $1,500.00)

A double-spurred handle makes this hot water pitcher, although simple, quite beautiful. Notice the colorful blue band around the rim and harp-shaped pattern surrounding the stenciled wildflower. This pitcher was part of a complete set as noted in the values above.

Shaving Mugs

Ribbed

Paneled Fir Tree   ### Bowtie

FOR ALL THREE EXAMPLES SHOWN:
SIZE: 4"h, 4"w
AVAILABILITY: Scarce
COLORS: Blue and white
MINT VALUE: $145.00 – $165.00

The Ribbed shaving mug at left, although simple in design, has excellent color. The very dark bands of blue diffuse in each direction to a white center. While the pattern is not very distinct, the vertical ribbing is discernable. Downward sweeping fir tree branches adorn the sides of the Paneled Fir Tree mug (above left). This pattern may be unique to shaving mugs as other pieces in the style are not currently known. The Bowtie pattern (above right) is commonly used for washstand and sanitation pieces. This shaving mug was likely a part of a complete set.

Basketweave and Morning Glory Chamber Pot

SIZE: 12"h (with lid), 9"w; lid, 10"w
AVAILABILITY: Rare pattern
COLORS: Blue and white
MINT VALUE: $425.00 – $475.00

The Basketweave and Morning Glory pattern is vivid and distinct on each side of this chamber pot. The lid also has the basketweave pattern with morning glories flanking each side of the handle. The wooden handled bail is original. The Basketweave and Morning Glory pattern is also used with a washstand set as presented earlier in this section.

Beaded Rose Cluster and Spear Points Chamber Pot
Fishscale and Wild Roses Chamber Pot

Left: Beaded Rose Cluster and Spear Points
        SIZE: 5½"h, 9¼"w
Right: Fishscale and Wild Roses
        SIZE: 4½"h, 7½"w
AVAILABILITY: Common pattern, rare small size
COLORS: Blue and White, Green and Cream
MINT VALUE: Large Beaded Rose Cluster: $175.00 – $200.00
            Small Fishscale and Wild Roses: $350.00 – $400.00

Large and small versions of two chamber pot patterns are provided for comparison. Both above and below, the larger Beaded Rose Cluster and Spear Points examples in blue and green appear at left while small Fishscale and Wild Roses examples are on the right. The smaller versions are the rare child's size. While the pattern is very faint, the green Beaded Rose Cluster example (below left) is quite rare.

Open Rose and Spear Point Panels Chamber Pot

SIZE: 5½"h, 9¼"w
AVAILABILITY: Common
COLORS: Blue and white
MINT VALUE: $150.00 – $175.00

This Open Rose and Spear Point Panels chamber pot has very light coloration and shallow pattern markings which, according to pricing guidelines, would diminish its value.

Scrolls Chamber Pot

SIZE: 10½"h (with lid), 9½"w; lid, 10"w
AVAILABILITY: Common
COLORS: Blue and white
MINT VALUE: $175.00 – $225.00

This Scrolls pattern chamberpot is very similar to one which includes a fleur-de-lis in the front center. Pale blue coloring is typical for this pattern. The lid is completely white.

Sponge with Blue Bands Chamber Pot

SIZE: 12"h (with lid), 9"w; lid, 9¾"w
AVAILABILITY: Extremely rare form
COLORS: Blue and white
MINT VALUE: $650.00 – $700.00

This lovely large sponge chamber pot has a unique shape and a nice triple blue band at its center. The original lid is domed and has a large center knob. It is quite rare to find a piece of this size in such excellent condition.

Sponge Child's Chamber Pot

SIZE: 4½"h, 7½"w
AVAILABILITY: Rare size
COLORS: Blue and white
MINT VALUE: $250.00 – $300.00

This is a child's chamber pot in close sponged blue.

Bear Paw Sponge with Blue Bands Chamber Pot

SIZE: 5"h, 8½"w
AVAILABILITY: Rare
COLORS: Blue and white
MINT VALUE: $250.00 – $275.00

This chamber pot has a center band of blue that attempts to be a triple band in places. The top and bottom are sponge decorated in a bear paw pattern which is larger than the earthworm design.

Cat Face Soap Dish

SIZES FOR ALL: 1"h, 4¼" – 5"w
AVAILABILITY: Scarce
COLORS: Blue and white generally, green and cream is extremely rare
MINT VALUE: $150.00 – $200.00 (for all shown except reproductions)
WARNING: Reproductions have been made

Wonderful color and excellent mold marks make this Cat Face soap dish a beauty.

Cat Face Soap Dish (Possible Reproduction)

Note the difference in the cat face in this reproduction piece. The back of the dish (right) looks old with the darkened edges. Beware of fakes purporting to be the real thing.

Fishscale and Wild Roses Soap Dish

Color and mold marks are excellent in this soap dish. Although not very visible, soap scum exists which will not turn loose. The back of this old piece has an indented lip which is typical of the real thing.

Flower Cluster and Fishscale Soap Dish

The soap dish at right has excellent dark blue color with a distinct flower pattern. Although the mold marks on the green dish at right are very faint, the rare green color makes it a worthy collectible.

Indian in War Bonnet Soap Dish

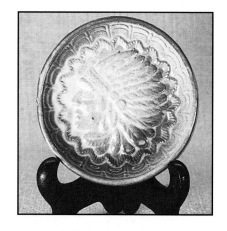

The soap dish at left above has wonderful color and an excellent pattern. You can literally count the feathers in the bonnet of the Indian who is surrounded by a zigzag medallion. The small chip on this example would, of course, reduce its value. The pattern on the center dish highlights the Indian more with a heavy white glaze which may denote a reproduction. The authenticity of this piece is further questioned on the back (at far right) since it is not off-set around the edge of the rim although it appears to look old. Authentic Indian in War Bonnet soap dishes typically command higher prices.

Lion's Head Soap Dish

The Lion's Head pattern is quite rare and typically commands higher prices. In this example, the mold of the lion's face is deep with good color. The back of this soap dish at right bears an off-set edge around the rim.

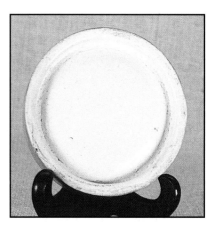

Rose in Beaded Medallion Soap Dish

An open rose is encircled by beads with lines radiating from the beads to the edge.

Stenciled Flower Soap Dish

A dark blue flower stencil has been applied to this dish. Notice the raised, concentric bands for draining of the soap bar.

Plain with Rose Transfer Soap Dish

This rectangular-shaped dish with sloping sides has an outer edge highlighted in dark blue. The middle is white with a centered small rose decal. Raised bars on each side of the decal provide elevation for drying of the soap.

Rectangular Sponge Soap Dish

The dark blue sponging is stunning. Raised bars are present for elevation of the soap.

Round Sponge Soap Dish

The closely sponged soap dish above is round with raised bands to elevate the soap.

The bottom of this dish is shown at right with the unglazed outer rim visible.

Footwarmers

These comparisons show the small size versus the large size footwarmers. Both are identical with the exception of the handle on the larger version. Note the dark lettering "PAT. APL'D FOR." Each piece also has the maker's mark (Logan Pottery Company, Logan, Ohio) on one end and "O.K. Foot Warmer" stamped on the opposite end.

LARGE SIZE: 12"l, 6¼"d; Handle 10¼"l
SMALL SIZE: 6"h, 3½"d
AVAILABILITY: Large, scarce; small, extremely rare
COLORS: Blue and white
MINT VALUES: Large: $275.00 – $350.00
                 Small: $750.00 – $800.00

The smaller version has been referred to both as a salesman's sample and as a handwarmer and is considered extremely rare.

SIZE: 10¾"l, 8"h
AVAILABILITY: Scarce
COLORS: Cream with blue lettering
MINT VALUE: $175.00 – $225.00

This footwarmer has a screw-on top for easier opening. The handle attaches to the top of the piece, and a pattern of spokes extends on each side. The dark blue marking appears on one side only. Notice the tri-purpose use of this item per the manufacturer's labeling.

∽——Water Bottle——∽

Not only is this a beautiful and rare piece, it is also a great conversation item. The manufacturer's name, Western Stoneware Co., as well as its intended use, are both molded in the bottom. These markings are quite rare in themselves. Note the excellent coloration and deep pattern. (Formerly from the collection of Ted and Sandra Gleason.)

SIZE: 10"l, 5½"d
AVAILABILITY: Extremely rare
COLORS: Blue and white
MINT VALUE: $500.00 – $750.00

Basketweave and Morning Glory Cuspidor

SIZE: 5"h, 7½"wd
AVAILABILITY: Scarce pattern
COLORS: Blue and white
MINT VALUE: $125.00 – $150.00

The Basketweave and Morning Glory pattern is a beauty on this cuspidor. The detail is deeply molded.

Bow and Shell Cuspidor

SIZE: 5"h, 7½"w
AVAILABILITY: Scarce pattern
COLORS: Blue and white
MINT VALUE: $125.00 – $150.00

This beautiful cuspidor has flowing ribbons and bows draped around the bulbous body. Each bow has a dropped shell from the center of the bow. The base is also surrounded by shells on an impressed dots background. The piece is further enhanced by the swirl pattern. Note that there are two examples shown. One has a deeper pattern and is a slate blue color.

Butterfly and Shield Cuspidor

SIZE: 6"h, 7½"w
AVAILABILITY: Rare pattern
COLORS: Blue and white
MINT VALUE: $175.00 – $225.00

Each arch around this cuspidor is centered with a small butterfly. The pattern is evenly carried to the upper rim. Scrolls and medallions complete the decoration.

Flower and Orange Peel Cuspidor

SIZE: 5"h, 7½"w
AVAILABILITY: Rare pattern
COLORS: Blue and white
MINT VALUE: $175.00 – $225.00

This cuspidor has an orange peel background. A stem of leaves and a flower circle the center of only one side.

Flower Panels and Arches Cuspidor

Flowers housed in graceful arches encompass the body and lip of this elegant piece. The larger flowers are accented by deep shades of blue. The interior rim (below) is highlighted by a diffused blue band.

SIZE: 7"h, 7½"w
AVAILABILITY: Rare pattern
COLORS: Blue and white
MINT VALUE: $250.00 – $300.00

Laurel Wreath Cuspidor

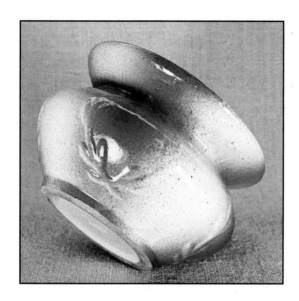

SIZE: 5"h, 7½"w
AVAILABILITY: Scarce pattern
COLORS: Blue and white
MINT VALUE: $175.00 – $225.00

Laurel wreaths appear on four sides of this cuspidor and are striped with dark blue, creating a nice color pattern.

Lilies and Plumes Cuspidor

SIZE: 5½"h, 7½"w
AVAILABILITY: Common pattern
COLORS: Blue and white, brown
MINT VALUES: Blue and white: $125.00 – $150.00
Brown: $75.00 – $125.00

A center cluster of lilies is surrounded by graceful plumes on both sides of this cuspidor. Although brown glazes are not the most colorful, this example has a rich golden color with light and dark variations. The Lilies and Plumes cuspidor was also produced in blue and white.

Orange Peel Cuspidor

SIZE: 5"h, 7½"w
AVAILABILITY: Common
COLORS: Blue and white
MINT VALUE: $125.00 – $150.00

Although void of a demonstrative pattern, this orange peel cuspidor is attractive with the upper and lower banding of blue hues.

Spongeware with Bands Cuspidor

SIZE: 5"h, 7½"w (sizes may vary)
AVAILABILITY: Common pattern
COLORS: Blue and white
MINT VALUE: $175.00 – $225.00

Cuspidors in sponge varied as much as the maker's imagination. It is difficult to find two exactly the same. Shown here are excellent examples of the form. Although commonly seen, all sponge commands higher prices, especially when in mint condition such as these pieces.

The earthworm pattern around the inner and outer rim and base of this blue-banded cuspidor makes it an especially attractive piece.

Tulip Jardiniere

SIZES: Pot: 6"h, 7"w
Pedestal: 7½"h, 6½"w
AVAILABILITY: Extremely rare
COLORS: Blue and white
MINT VALUE: $1,200.00 – $1,500.00

This lovely set was actually bought on separate occasions, according to its owner. The base unit was purchased from someone who did not know of its use. Both are in mint condition and are a perfect color match. The pedestal and pot are the same on each side. Bouquets of tulips center the design with a background of raised lines that appear to be grass blades. The bottom of the pot fits securely in a raised rim on the top of the pedestal. Although not shown, the pedestal's bottom and top have a one-inch hole in the center. Jardinieres were also produced in the Cosmos and Apple Blossom patterns.

Planter

SIZE: 7½"h, 9"w
AVAILABILITY: Rare
COLORS: Blue and white
MINT VALUE: $250.00 – $275.00

This rare hanging planter is highlighted with speckled blue diffusing that fades to white toward the bottom. There is an interior draining hole. Since it is not a free-standing piece, the wide collar would have held the planter in a stand or it could have been hung by chains or rope which could be attached to the three holes around the top.

Vase

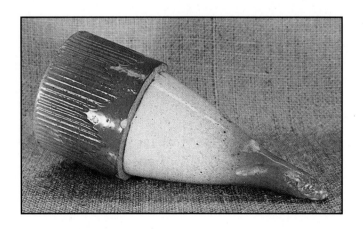

SIZE: 9½"h, 4"d
AVAILABILITY: Rare
COLORS: Blue and white
MINT VALUE: $250.00 – $275.00

This unusual piece is a vase used for grave flowers. The tapered end would have been placed in the ground. The open end would have held a bouquet of flowers probably placed in water for special occasions.

Deer in the Woods Sand Jar

SIZE: 15"h, 12"w
AVAILABILITY: Extremely rare
COLORS: Solid green
MINT VALUE: $800.00 – $1,000.00

This highly detailed work of art reflects a wooded scene with grazing buck and doe. The authenticity of the wood-scape makes one almost smell the fresh fir trees. Both sides are entirely different. One has the buck and doe in the woods; the other is a grove of trees. Note the bottom center of the photo at right; the small circle shows where a spout may have been attached had this piece been made into a water cooler rather than a sand jar for disposal of cigarette butts.

Gothic Windows Umbrella Stand

SIZE: 18"h, 9¼"w
AVAILABILITY: Extremely rare
COLORS: Green and cream
MINT VALUE: $800.00 – $1,000.00

This Gothic Windows pattern umbrella stand features windows accented with green at the top and bottom. The center has vertical columns connecting a reverse pattern at the base.

Iris Umbrella Stand

SIZE: 20"h, 11"w
AVAILABILITY: Extremely rare
COLORS: Green and cream
MINT VALUE: $1,200.00 – $1,500.00

This is the perfect umbrella stand. Dark green bands adorn the top and bottom with a lattice pattern. The top portion also features a band of roping detail and small flowers. The mid-section of cream iris makes this a truly spectacular piece.

Patterns Index

Forms Index

End Notes

1. *American Potters and Pottery*, John Ramsay. Tudor Publishing Company, New York, NY, 1947.

2. *Blue & White Stoneware*, Kathryn McNerney. Collector Books, Paducah, KY, 1981.

3. "Blue-and-White Stoneware Now More Popular Than Ever," William Daggett, *AntiqueWeek*, Eastern Edition, May 29, 1995, pg. 2.

4. "Collecting the Best — Spatter and Sponge," Karla Klein Albertson, *Early American Life*, April 1989.

5. *Collector's Guide to Country Stoneware & Pottery, Second Series,* Don & Carol Raycraft. Collector Books, Paducah, KY, 1990.

6. *Collector's Guide to Country Stoneware & Pottery,* Don & Carol Raycraft. Collector Books, Paducah, KY, 1985.

7. "Discovery of Photos Sheds New Light on Logan Pottery," James L. Murphy, *AntiqueWeek*, Eastern Edition, July 17, 1995, pg. 15.

8. *Early American Folk Pottery,* Harold F. Guilland. Chitton Book Company, Philadelphia, PA, 1971.

9. *The History of American Ceramics 1607 to Present,* Elaine Levin. Harry N. Abrams, Inc., Publishers, New York, NY, 1988.

10. *Our Pioneer Potters,* Arthur W. Clement. Z. Smith Reynolds Library, Wake Forest University, Winston-Salem, NC, 1947.

11. *Red Wing Stoneware,* Dan & Gail DePasquale & Larry Peterson. Collector Books, Paducah, KY, 1983.

12. "Spongeware," Mimi Handler, *Early American Life*, October 1992.

13. "Sunday Best (Splatterware)," Linda Joan Smith, *Country Home*, April 1993.

14. "There is More to Logan Pottery Than Just Blue and White," Forrest Poston, *AntiqueWeek*, Eastern Edition, July 17, 1995, pg. 15.

15. *Yellow Ware: The Transitional Ceramic*, Joan Leibowitz. Schiffer Publishing Ltd., Atglen, PA, 1985.

COLLECTOR BOOKS

I n f o r m i n g   T o d a y ' s   C o l l e c t o r

*For over two decades we have been keeping collectors informed
on trends and values in all fields of antiques and collectibles.*

BOOKS ON GLASS AND POTTERY

1810	American Art Glass, Shuman	$29.95
1312	Blue & White Stoneware, McNerney	$9.95
1959	Blue Willow, 2nd Ed., Gaston	$14.95
3719	Coll. Glassware from the 40's, 50's, 60's, 2nd Ed., Florence	$19.95
3816	Collectible Vernon Kilns, Nelson	$24.95
3311	Collecting Yellow Ware – Id. & Value Gd., McAllister	$16.95
1373	Collector's Ency. of American Dinnerware, Cunningham	$24.95
3815	Coll. Ency. of Blue Ridge Dinnerware, Newbound	$19.95
2272	Collector's Ency. of California Pottery, Chipman	$24.95
3811	Collector's Ency. of Colorado Pottery, Carlton	$24.95
3312	Collector's Ency. of Children's Dishes, Whitmyer	$19.95
2133	Collector's Ency. of Cookie Jars, Roerig	$24.95
3723	Coll. Ency. of Cookie Jars-Volume II, Roerig	$24.95
3724	Collector's Ency. of Depression Glass, 11th Ed., Florence	$19.95
2209	Collector's Ency. of Fiesta, 7th Ed., Huxford	$19.95
1439	Collector's Ency. of Flow Blue China, Gaston	$19.95
3812	Coll. Ency. of Flow Blue China, 2nd Ed., Gaston	$24.95
3813	Collector's Ency. of Hall China, 2nd Ed., Whitmyer	$24.95
2334	Collector's Ency. of Majolica Pottery, Katz-Marks	$19.95
1358	Collector's Ency. of McCoy Pottery, Huxford	$19.95
3313	Collector's Ency. of Niloak, Gifford	$19.95
3837	Collector's Ency. of Nippon Porcelain I, Van Patten	$24.95
2089	Collector's Ency. of Nippon Porcelain II, Van Patten	$24.95
1665	Collector's Ency. of Nippon Porcelain III, Van Patten	$24.95
1447	Collector's Ency. of Noritake, 1st Series, Van Patten	$19.95
1034	Collector's Ency. of Roseville Pottery, Huxford	$19.95
1035	Collector's Ency. of Roseville Pottery, 2nd Ed., Huxford	$19.95
3314	Collector's Ency. of Van Briggle Art Pottery, Sasicki	$24.95
3433	Collector's Guide To Harker Pottery - U.S.A., Colbert	$17.95
2339	Collector's Guide to Shawnee Pottery, Vanderbilt	$19.95
1425	Cookie Jars, Westfall	$9.95
3440	Cookie Jars, Book II, Westfall	$19.95
2275	Czechoslovakian Glass & Collectibles, Barta	$16.95
3882	Elegant Glassware of the Depression Era, 6th Ed., Florence	$19.95
3725	Fostoria - Pressed, Blown & Hand Molded Shapes, Kerr	$24.95
3883	Fostoria Stemware - The Crystal for America, Long	$24.95
3886	Kitchen Glassware of the Depression Years, 5th Ed., Florence	$19.95
3889	Pocket Guide to Depression Glass, 9th Ed., Florence	$9.95
3825	Puritan Pottery, Morris	$24.95
1670	Red Wing Collectibles, DePasquale	$9.95
1440	Red Wing Stoneware, DePasquale	$9.95
1958	So. Potteries Blue Ridge Dinnerware, 3rd Ed., Newbound	$14.95
3739	Standard Carnival Glass, 4th Ed., Edwards	$24.95
3327	Watt Pottery – Identification & Value Guide, Morris	$19.95
2224	World of Salt Shakers, 2nd Ed., Lechner	$24.95

BOOKS ON DOLLS & TOYS

2079	Barbie Fashion, Vol. 1, 1959-1967, Eames	$24.95
3310	Black Dolls – 1820 - 1991 - Id. & Value Guide, Perkins	$17.95
3810	Chatty Cathy Dolls, Lewis	$15.95
1529	Collector's Ency. of Barbie Dolls, DeWein	$19.95
2338	Collector's Ency. of Disneyana, Longest & Stern	$24.95
3727	Coll. Guide to Ideal Dolls, Izen	$18.95
3822	Madame Alexander Price Guide #19, Smith	$9.95
3732	Matchbox Toys, 1948 to 1993, Johnson	$18.95
3733	Modern Collector's Dolls, 6th series, Smith	$24.95
1540	Modern Toys, 1930 - 1980, Baker	$19.95
3824	Patricia Smith's Doll Values – Antique to Modern, 10th ed.	$12.95
3826	Story of Barbie, Westenhouser, No Values	$19.95
2028	Toys, Antique & Collectible, Longest	$14.95
1808	Wonder of Barbie, Manos	$9.95
1430	World of Barbie Dolls, Manos	$9.95

OTHER COLLECTIBLES

1457	American Oak Furniture, McNerney	$9.95
3716	American Oak Furniture, Book II, McNerney	$12.95
2333	Antique & Collectible Marbles, 3rd Ed., Grist	$9.95
1748	Antique Purses, Holiner	$19.95
1426	Arrowheads & Projectile Points, Hothem	$7.95
1278	Art Nouveau & Art Deco Jewelry, Baker	$9.95
1714	Black Collectibles, Gibbs	$19.95
1128	Bottle Pricing Guide, 3rd Ed., Cleveland	$7.95
3717	Christmas Collectibles, 2nd Ed., Whitmyer	$24.95
1752	Christmas Ornaments, Johnston	$19.95
3718	Collectible Aluminum, Grist	$16.95
2132	Collector's Ency. of American Furniture, Vol. I, Swedberg	$24.95
2271	Collector's Ency. of American Furniture, Vol. II, Swedberg	$24.95
3720	Coll. Ency. of American Furniture, Vol III, Swedberg	$24.95
3722	Coll. Ency. of Compacts, Carryalls & Face Powder Boxes, Mueller	$24.95
2018	Collector's Ency. of Granite Ware, Greguire	$24.95
3430	Coll. Ency. of Granite Ware, Book 2, Greguire	$24.95
1441	Collector's Guide to Post Cards, Wood	$9.95
2276	Decoys, Kangas	$24.95
1716	Fifty Years of Fashion Jewelry, Baker	$19.95
3817	Flea Market Trader, 9th Ed., Huxford	$12.95
3731	Florence's Standard Baseball Card Price Gd., 6th Ed.	$9.95
3819	General Store Collectibles, Wilson	$24.95
3436	Grist's Big Book of Marbles, Everett Grist	$19.95
2278	Grist's Machine Made & Contemporary Marbles	$9.95
1424	Hatpins & Hatpin Holders, Baker	$9.95
3884	Huxford's Collectible Advertising – Id. & Value Gd., 2nd Ed	$24.95
3820	Huxford's Old Book Value Guide, 6th Ed.	$19.95
3821	Huxford's Paperback Value Guide	$19.95
1181	100 Years of Collectible Jewelry, Baker	$9.95
2216	Kitchen Antiques – 1790 - 1940, McNerney	$14.95
3887	Modern Guns – Id. & Val. Gd., 10th Ed., Quertermous	$12.95
3734	Pocket Guide to Handguns, Quertermous	$9.95
3735	Pocket Guide to Rifles, Quertermous	$9.95
3736	Pocket Guide to Shotguns, Quertermous	$9.95
2026	Railroad Collectibles, 4th Ed., Baker	$14.95
1632	Salt & Pepper Shakers, Guarnaccia	$9.95
1888	Salt & Pepper Shakers II, Guarnaccia	$14.95
2220	Salt & Pepper Shakers III, Guarnaccia	$14.95
3443	Salt & Pepper Shakers IV, Guarnaccia	$18.95
3890	Schroeder's Antiques Price Guide, 13th Ed.	$14.95
2096	Silverplated Flatware, 4th Ed., Hagan	$14.95
2348	20th Century Fashionable Plastic Jewelry, Baker	$19.95
3828	Value Guide to Advertising Memorabilia, Summers	$18.95
3830	Vintage Vanity Bags & Purses, Gerson	$24.95

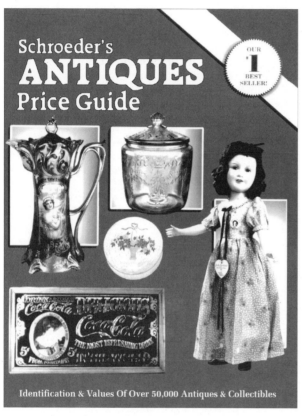